American
CEOs
Can do better, we have the technology?

American CEOs
Can do better, we have the technology?

✦

The American high & low intellectual property is
at risk for terrorism from abroad.

Wayne Holovacs Ph.D., MBA, BS
"Dr. Wayne"

iUniverse, Inc.

New York Lincoln Shanghai

American CEOs Can do better, we have the technology?
The American high & low intellectual property is at risk for terrorism from abroad.

iUniverse books may be ordered through booksellers or by contacting:

iUniverse
2021 Pine Lake Road, Suite 100
Lincoln, NE 68512
www.iuniverse.com
1-800-Authors (1-800-288-4677)

ISBN-13: 978-0-595-35163-3 (pbk)
ISBN-13: 978-0-595-67208-0 (cloth)
ISBN-13: 978-0-595-79862-9 (ebk)
ISBN-10: 0-595-35163-8 (pbk)
ISBN-10: 0-595-67208-6 (cloth)
ISBN-10: 0-595-79862-4 (ebk)

Printed in the United States of America

Contents

There is little time left to regain the balance of Out-souring American technology. Corporate CEOs giving educational monies abroad and choking off the country they and their families live in, America.

Out-sourcing and In-sourcing is good…if…if…it is in balance and fair, however, it is our American CEOs, and the American government with its elected officials that share this responsibility. they will ultimately make this choice, and the decision. today In 2005 President George W. Bush is taking steps forward, yes, the U.S. government and a few CEOs are taking action, but it may be to slow or to late. You decide? There is help on the way…the help is you, the American citizens with our American CEOs and what God given inalienable rights we have been given, the American Constitution, and being an American citizen allows us what rights to have. Remember we are at war with Terrorism and what does that have to do with anything?

Is this the best our **American CEOs** can do?

By Wayne Holovacs, Ph.D., MBA, BS (Dr. Wayne)

Acknowledgments

Thank you to my family, Carol, Benjamin and Nicholas for their love and helpfulness, in helping me with this subject "**American CEOs** can do better we have the technology?". The research staff of Dr. Wayne at **_TPOR_** as always continues to be fair and balanced in their tireless work to bring the facts out on Out-sourcing and In-sourcing high and low technologies world-wide (with hands-on experiences themselves), even when they didn't know what the facts would reveal.

I want to say a special thank you just for being there when I needed you. My thanks to Pauline Holovacs, Brad Holovacs, John Morton, Warren Smith, Rodney (Rod) Labby, Robert Moreland, Michael Neuffer, Rob Robinson, Charlie Eicher, Ron McRae, Robert Murphy, Barry Hughes, Jim McKay, Leroy L. Davis, Calvin Cheung, John Morton, Rick Eldridge, Adrienne Roberts, Rene Martineze, Mike Banta, Jim Evans, Robert Roth, Belle Cooper, Cindy Cox, Don Long, Manish Asthana, Anna Huynh and Herman Wong and Carl Johnson.

All of us are fortunate to be a part of "real-people" whom have worked directly with Out-sourcing and In-sourcing, high tech and low tech products and services in multiple industries. Americans are committed to ensuring America's high and low technology resource interests, its "intellectual property" the

Human-Resource which is key in providing world-class products and services, but most important keeping the-free-world safe from terrorism through technology awareness. My thanks as well to iUniverse, Inc., who believed this subject of "**American CEOs** can do better we have the technology?", Out-sourcing American technology and American intellectual property was so important that it deserved to be a book.

*For globalization to work for America, the world econo-
mies must work for working people. We must first measure
the success of our economy (America) by the American
middle class, and the scope of opportunity offered to the
poorest child to climb into that middle class and beyond.*

—WAYNE HOLOVACS

*We frequently see the respectful attentions of the world
more strongly directed towards the rich and the great and
the powerful than towards the wise and the virtuous. We
see frequently more and more vices and the follies of the
powerful than the poverty and weakness of the innocents of
our children.*

—DR. WAYNE

Introduction

The power of big business over our national American life has never been greater. Never have there been fewer business leaders (CEOs) willing to commit to the American national interest over selfish interest, for the good of the country, over that of the companies they lead. Just look at the news on television. What say you about the "Martha Stewart Omni-media™ company, and although Martha Stewart was the CEO, convicted of a federal crime and went to jail, will most likely be back as the CEO in about two years time," says *News-media*. How does a parent explain that outcome to their children. And the indifference of many technology business leaders to our long-term national welfare is nowhere more evident than in the Out-sourcing of American intellectual property and American jobs because of "cheap-cost-labor", overseas labor markets", rather than utilizing a balanced and fair trade agreement, which makes for fair trade, and a living standard that is beneficial for all throughout the world. The rising debate over Out-sourcing of hundreds of thousands of American jobs, American knowledge, American "High & Low Technology", "its intellectual property" has revealed a fundamental imbalance in our economy, and society of scale, but of which can be regained and its composure ensured again…if so desired by our American CEOs. This debate has exposed an altogether too uncomfortable alliance between multinational corporations lack of governess, that is "being a good corporate citizen" and a balance of governments, which has resulted in Corporate America's dominance over Washington law makers in many areas. I must say though, in the same breath, that with the current American administration, President George W. Bush seems to be taking aim at the scope of this problem and directing efforts to balance and grow in a fair direction. We will have to wait and see…This subject **"American CEOs** can do better we have the technology is to focus our attention on U.S. trade policies and to many American CEOs that haven't worked to there most effective state for three decades, since I was 10 years old. And, most important, it has raised the question of whether will continue to freely offer American Technology for manufacturer overseas and sacrifice a balancing of American jobs, our middle-class, our national wealth, but most importantly America's safety…remember America is in a global war on terrorism and it is affecting Corporate America's (American CEOs) pursuit of fair international trade agreements that should be "free, fair and balanced trade". The resolution of American CEOs and the CEO decisions that are made will ultimately determine whether our middle-class will continue to diminish or will once again flourish, or will America enact harsh laws to ensure that American CEOs play by the rules of **"fair-play"**. Is America a country that works only for the wealthy and powerful? or will she insist on forging a future in which America works for all of us. And at this moment, the outcome is far from assured while American families are hurting. Motives behind these kinds of decision makers are not meant to be destructive if fair and balanced trade is established either by want, by will, or by law. Simply put without fair and balanced global trade all our ways of life will become troubling and painful and yes, it will have a global effect. My criticism of this relatively recent, but rapidly growing corporate practice of shipping American jobs to "cheap-cost-labor" foreign labor markets is at the serious point. Accused of being about working men and women in this country "America" does not tell the full story, it is much more for a CEO to say that the United States must be ferociously competitive in our global economy is an aggressive strategy, true, but one that has been common place for decades, that's why America is the economic leader. Yes, I know and heard a few American corporate CEOs have even been called a communist, even a "Witch" and some government officials in the American Congress say this sounds like being a protectionist issue.

We Americans are not stupid...we know that both communism and being a protectionist is not beneficial, However, we must consider that there is a cause and affect without fair and balance global trade, and we must turn away from "unbalanced-trade" at seemingly any cost to workers and our (American) economy & safety.

Some folks are being accused of being a raving populist, but remember free and open debate makes for good decision making (sometimes). I'm not always sure which of those slurs though is intended to be the worst, but it doesn't help matters now does it?

Of course, the word "intimidation" comes up and is precisely the desired effect of those, slurs, and, in some cases, outright personal attacks that many American CEOs are held responsible and maybe they should be...and what about our children? As often happens in our lives, unintended consequences have a way of winning-out, or do they? That's because instead of being intimidated, **American CEOs** can do better we have the technology? And employee's are not communicating effectively. Is it pride stopping the discussions and working to agree on a fair and balanced solution?

Its easy to cut-head count, any CEO can do that, that is the CEO of the past and a few still sit...the non-thinkers. What happened to creative ideas? American values are changing, but in which direction?

Since 9/11 the American people for a while came together as a country, even after such a horrible event, but Americans will do that, its in all of our spirits, including American CEOs.

Today it seems as though where moving father apart and this is a frustrating time...blue states, red states...such unrest, fair and balanced American CEOs wanting to make improvements are simply afraid to act being of the minority. Driving in my car I recently seen a very large bill-board that had two name's on it side-by-side, maybe there is hope? "**Bush Sr. and Clinton**". Remember this is March 2005.

Try a simple test: Ask people you meet, friends, family, colleagues...simply, and in general...What do you think about American CEOs? Out-sourcing? Or do you like In-sourcing? or would a more fair and balanced approach or method with consensus in place be better? You will not be surprised with the responses. Just my point. Although, depending on weather you ask an American citizen verses a Non-American citizen, be prepared for a surprise or even be prepared to protect yourself, ouch!

Just an example, sometimes critics in business, government, and the media will attack a spokes person but not the real-issue, why is that? Instead of trying to refute arguments with facts and reason. Why should American CEOs do better? Because many American CEOs continue to be in Crisis and afraid to act and do the right thing. Is it acting out incorrectly and without concern for America, is that the reason? Will Americans continue to lose their jobs, and American CEOs keep giving away its technology without good reason? Could it be for no other reason than they were making a decent living and couldn't compete with someone in China, India, or Eastern Europe who earned a fraction of their wages. And on too many occasions, their (American CEOs) not only laid them (employees) off, but then forced them to train their overseas replacements. I still can't understand how anyone could treat a person, a coworker and colleague-a fellow American-like that. Of course, there's a lot about Outsourcing that requires some-work to understand, its not so simple. Even after researching the subject from every conceivable angle, I still find it difficult to accept that so many leaders of Corporate America, American CEOs could descend to such a level that they would ship American jobs and technologies without proper controls overseas to achieve what are at best relatively insignificant cost reductions, while ignoring the pain of their employees and their families, and the burdens that Out-sourcing imposes on the communities in which their corporations do business.

Remember, "America and the world is at war with terrorism!"

I believe deeply in our free-enterprise democracy. I believe in the strength and resilience of this great economy of ours. I've not only been a recognized global expert in two industry's and technologies for two decades but also an executive, a businessman, and an investor. I understand business cycles and the harsh necessity of cutting expenses and laying off employees in down-cycles and up-cycles, as well as recessions. But I also know the importance of people, of employees and the need to invest in them.

It is the people that are the company, period! I know the importance of taking a longer view of business cycles, and a broader view of the responsibility owed by business and business leaders, not only to their investors but to all the stakeholders in the corporation, including employees, the community, and our country, America, the home of the free and the land of the brave.

I strongly believe that corporations should be good citizens. I also confess to being something of an optimist. America is far from perfect, but I have put my life on the line for America. I have served my country proudly in the U.S. Navy and I am proud to have served. We Americans enjoy a way of life unparalleled in history. Like most Americans, I'm a beneficiary of that way of life and have a deep sense of indebtedness to all who've made my good fortune possible. I was born into a working-class family and we were very poor, we made our own noodles, but they were delicious. We had happiness and joy, and never felt truly poor, because we had love and support at home and went to public schools, Church, Roosevelt School #10 where teachers took the time and interest to nurture all students, no matter their families' wealth or lack of it. And I was taught to respect anyone who worked for a living, and to respect my elders, no matter what the job or how much it paid. And to appreciate having a job. And my wife and I have passed that along to our children.

I know firsthand the importance of a strong public education and a job in achieving the American Dream, in ensuring for all Americans the opportunity to build a better life than that of their parents. Ask my mother. And it does bother me when I hear an American CEO, a lobbyist, or a politician say they support Out-sourcing jobs overseas because "Americans aren't well enough educated or sufficiently productive, or even claim that GOD himself said a job is not a GOD given right". I don't believe it's true. It's as we say in Texas "Bull-crap". Perhaps some American CEOs sincerely believe what they're saying. But even so, why don't they feel a sense of responsibility to keep workers here employed, to allow their taxes to finance better schools, to invest in the people who will build America's future? Maybe some people in Corporate America (CEOs) and some Politicians have forgotten about the American dream that should be the birthright of everyone in this country called: America.

I hope that after reading this book you'll take time to remind them of the American dream, your dream, and a fair and balanced trade agreement in this global economy. And help keep the American dream alive, or like my grandmother would have said, she passed away in 1963: "If you don't love America, and your freedom, leave…". You see my grandmother came from the "previous" Soviet Union.

1

Middle-Class American's down, but not out...

"The twentieth century has been characterized by five developments of great political importance: the growth of democracy, the growth of freedom and liberty, growth of corporate power, and the growth of corporate propaganda as a means at times of protecting corporate power against democracy."

—WAYNE HOLOVACS

The odds are that during the past recession, you or someone you know was affected by corporate layoffs and the loss of a high or low technology good paying job here in America. It's a painful experience, and one that can have a devastating effect on individuals and families. But in some cases, layoffs have affected entire towns, in effect crippling communities. And layoffs related to Out-sourcing have long-term effects on those communities, because companies pulling out take their taxes with them, that is, if they paid them at all, (sometimes a goodwill-offer is made and the corporation has a reduced local tax rate, it is meant to build-up communities and create new/more jobs.)

The people in the town, however, are unable to pay taxes, because they're no longer getting paid to work. Corporate pull-outs run the gamut from manufacturing low to high-tech products. "The examples in the next few pages are just a few of the scenarios that are playing out with alarming regularity in communities all across America. "In 2004 Syracuse, New York, Carrier, the maker of air conditioning and heating units, is closing two of its most productive and profitable factories and laying off 1,300 workers. Most of those jobs are headed to Singapore and Malaysia. It's too early for many of Carrier's employees to retire-the average worker at the plant is only forty-eight years old. In a move to save the jobs, New York State and the plant's union tried to change Carrier's decision (CEO) from Out-sourcing the jobs to Asia by offering a $42 million incentive package. To no avail-the company has Out-sourced these jobs." American CEOs in Crisis...?

...Today with the closing of the Carrier plant, central New York State has now lost 11,000 jobs since 1990. Senator Hillary Clinton was quoted as saying she believes "Manufacturing is not a luxury. It's not an old-fashioned economic activity." I am not sure what that means...

Design and manufacturing are core components of what we need to do to maintain a strong economy, and a strong national defense. Syracuse may be better off than some cities in that it has a bedrock industry: Higher Education. It's home to Syracuse University, and the city officials have worked hard to diversify its economy in the wake of Carriers CEO decision for Outsourcing those jobs. But there was more to come "when the cuts came" there were more plant closings by General Motors, General Electric, and Allied Signal. However, even with the bedrock of Syracuse University, wage growth in the city has fallen below the national average as manufacturing jobs have left, and unless these companies want to take a step towards fair and balanced trade and return to Syracuse these jobs will not be coming back.

What's happening in Syracuse may or may not be different from what is happening in many communities across America, it simply comes down to the decision by its CEO. From steel to appliances to automobiles, good paying manufacturing jobs are being Out-sourceed out of the country, leaving behind workers and communities struggling with how to recover. Many families simply leaving, never to return, and only left to remember their lives as they were and what happened.

The automobile industry is a prime example of a business in which "blood-letting pressure" to cut costs has driven jobs abroad. And it affects jobs in many states, called the trickle down effect. At Tower Automotive in Milwaukee, more than 550 employees used to make the frames for Dodge Ram pickup trucks. Now that work, and their jobs, are in Mexico. The decision was made by DaimlerChrysler's CEO, which is squeezing its American suppliers by asking them to match the lower wage prices available from overseas manufacturers. All the automakers, not just Chrysler, claim they need these lower prices in order to keep making affordable cars and to keep market share.

Early this year, Ford closed its plant in Edison, New Jersey, after more than **fifty-six years** of producing cars and trucks there. A Ford spokesman said it would be too expensive to retool that plant so that it could produce different models. About 375 of the plant's 905 workers were forced to early retirement, while others were transferred to Ford plants elsewhere in the country, which seemed to show some caring. Most notable though was, at least 450 jobs were eliminated. Ford is, however, investing heavily in Asia and has set up a new regional headquarters in Thailand.

General Motors, long the symbol of Detroit's automotive strength, has introduced a new Chevy, the Equinox in 2004. The Equinox is assembled in Canada with a Chinese made engine. Well that's a global trade process, right? Now, the three most expensive parts of any automobile are the body, engine, and transmission. With the Equinox featuring a foreign-built engine, more than a third of the vehicle's cost is being trans-ferred-and paid out-to China and not to American suppliers or workers. What say you? An interesting statistic: Employment in the U.S. auto industry has dropped by 250,000 jobs over the past four years. During that same time, imports of Chinese auto parts have doubled.

What makes all these examples so frustrating for American workers is that while Detroit throttles back at home and invests in Asia, foreign automakers, including Honda, Nissan, and Toyota, are investing in this market. In fact, as American auto-makers cut back, these Japanese companies (CEOs) are provid-ing all the production growth in the United States, global trade, right? And calling our American automakers the Big Three is now an Un-truth. Only two companies, Ford and GM, are American-based, while Chrysler is owned by German manufacturer DaimlerChrysler. To put a fine point on it with a number two pencil, Toyota is selling more cars in the United States than Chrysler. And Toyota is now the second leading global car company, after General Motors. Why? **It manufactures products were it sells them.**

We're not faring well in the auto business, and we're not faring well in the appliance business either. Galesburg, Illinois for twenty five years was home to a large Maytag factory. In fact, Galesburg was a Maytag company town, and Maytag provided 1,700 jobs to local workers. But Maytag's CEO decided to close its Galesburg factory and move much of the work to a new refrigerator manufacturing plant in Reynosa, Mexico. None of the American jobs are slated to be transferred-all 1,700 are scheduled to be laid off. Employees who made $15 an hour are being replaced by Mexican workers who earn less than $1 an hour, this begs the question of work-ethics and what is slave-labor? Maytag justifies the closing by citing competition from cheap-cost labor Asian refrigerators, and the tighter wallets of cost-conscious consumers. With a current jobless rate of 11 percent, Galesburg will soon face a possible unemployment rate of 23 percent, along with a very uncertain future. People there can't turn to the government for help. After all, free-trade agreements signed by the government promised workers at plants like this one a chance to Out-source their products to new markets around the world. But the reality is, the only thing being

Out-sourceed from Galesburg is American jobs and technologies.

Clintwood, Virginia, has a population of 1,958. It's not a big town, but 456 of its best jobs are in the process of being Out-sourced to India. Online travel service Travelocity is shutting down its call-center here. Workers at Travelocity made a starting wage of $8 an hour, slightly above minimum wage, plus training and benefits. But Travelocity lost $55 million last year and was looking to cut costs fast. Its CEO decided it could save $10 million by moving its Clintwood call-center to India.

Some caring, Travelocity is trying to give workers a soft landing by providing eleven months' notice, along with possible interviews at Travelocity's two remaining U.S. call-centers. Clintwood, meanwhile, is going back to its roots, marketing one of the few things that can't be Out-sourced: *tourism*. Combined with local crafts and a mountain music museum dedicated to a local artist, Grammy Award winner Ralph Stanley, the town is attracting attention. As a foot note, the whole Travelocity deal was felt like a stinging rash to Clintwood. Just before Travelocity set up shop there, Nexus Communications had shut down a similar call-center operation in the town.

Let's mention the people of Celina, Tennessee, who have experienced firsthand the cost of free but unfair and non-balanced trade. Thirteen hundred people once worked in the town's OshKosh plant in Celina.

Now **only ten do**. The rest of those American jobs were sent out of the country, to Mexico and Honduras. Some of the company's employees had worked at OshKosh for more than three decades. But with OshKosh gone, the unemployment rate in Celina is 17.5 percent, and its per capita income has fallen to $10,500. While Celina is just one more town abandoned by American companies in search of cheap-cost-cost foreign labor, the town is fighting to get back on its feet and stay there. A star, Clay County has created a Web site to attract new business to Celina and the surrounding area, and the chamber of commerce is aggressively selling the county to outsiders. It has already been successful, having lured a commonly Out-sourced business to the town: **a call-center**. Healthcare Management Resources has set up a new center to handle billing for hospitals and now employs 129 people. The jobs don't pay as much as the factory jobs at OshKosh, but it's steady work and it carries benefits. Moreover, the company is thrilled with Celina. According to Mr. Dennis Swartz, the president of Healthcare Management Resources, the people of Celina have a "great work ethic. I put these people up against anybody anywhere. And my goal in life is really to set up a third center, a fourth center, a **fifth** center in areas just like this."

Internet provider Earth-link is closing its call-center in Harrisburg, Pennsylvania, and sending 476 jobs to the Philippines and India. The state of Pennsylvania has already been hard hit by job losses, having seen 148,000 manufacturing jobs evaporate. Now it's seeing its high-tech jobs go away fast. At a stop in Harrisburg in 2004, President George W. Bush told Pennsylvanians that "There are people looking for work because jobs have gone overseas. And we need to act in this country. We need to act to make sure there are more jobs at home." Today its starting to turn around, but very slowly.

Outside of the obvious factory closings and new call-centers in India, there are the insidious under-the-radar-scope cases of Out-sourcing and technology manufacturing transfers that we rarely ever detect. They eat away at our economic infrastructure like termites in your house, and we barely notice-until it's too late. An example, The Smithsonian Institution chose Innodata Isogen to create an online library of one of the most expansive research projects in American history, the United States Exploring Expedition.

Running from 1838 to 1843, it was the first federally funded mission of exploration in U.S. history and yielded over 3,000 pages of data on topics including, anthropology, American art, geology and more. But, Innodata Isogen Out-sourced the work to the Philippines. According to the Smithsonian, "the work was sent overseas because there are not enough skilled workers in this country to do the job. Well what do you think of that...**Technology is becoming extinct in America?**", American CEOs in Crisis? I find it incredibly hard to believe that it required Out-sourcing talent to chronicle the legacy of one of America's greatest research endeavors, but I could be wrong?

Under-the-radar-scope Out-sourcing affects small industries that have been the source of jobs in the United States for as long as most people can remember. The embroidery industry, of which my mother worked for a time, when I was a young lad, one of the mainstays of the New Jersey economy for more than a century, is now in danger of disappearing from this country.

Small New Jersey factories once made 90 percent of the embroidery in American lingerie, clothing, and bedding. It was a half-billion-dollar-a-year industry with nearly 8,500 jobs. Today, there are less than 850 jobs left. American clothing manufacturers still require embroidery on their products, but they've gone to Sri Lanka, India, China, and Mexico to get it done.

It's doubtful that anyone will claim that embroidery is a critical component of our national economy, or high-tech security concern, yet it is a traditional craft that has provided a good income to thousands of Americans for generations. And there's still a lot of it being done-just not by Americans. It's one more part of apparel manufacturing that is being Out-sourced. Today, 98.5 percent of clothing production is done outside our borders. That fact had a direct bearing on last year's closing of thirty-eight textile factories in North and South Carolina alone.

And when it comes to apparel, even gaping loopholes in U.S. Customs inspections of clothing and textiles are costing American jobs. Less than one-tenth of one percent of the three million textile shipments that come into this country every year are inspected. That's a security gap that foreign textile manufacturers have been exploiting to their benefit and our detriment. Knowing that they are unlikely to get caught, unscrupulous producers will label a piece of clothing to read that it was made in, say, Honduras, when it may actually have come from China. Then it's shipped to the United States using falsified entry documents, according to a recent General Accounting Office report, the lack of inspection at our borders results in the frequent smuggling of garments past U.S. customs. If you look at every one of these companies, industries, towns, and communities, Out-sourcing has far-reaching and devastating effects across all aspects of our society, because of unfair and non-balanced global trade practices. Yet there is still one more insidious element: the growing multibillion-dollar industry made up of companies that are actually getting paid to help other companies Out-source their businesses. Many of the companies who want jobs to go to cheap-cost-labor foreign labor markets are not doing it by themselves, and there are a lot of consultants anxious to help.

U.S. businesses spent $16 billion on Out-sourcing work last year, according to leading IT research company Gartner Inc. But Out-sourcing overseas often means that corporations have to rely on consulting firms that specialize in Out-sourcing. Consultants often play a role as the middle-man or middle-woman, connecting companies with offshore providers and holding conferences to help companies Out-source and "off-shore" work. This year 2005, at a New York City hotel, corporate executives paid more than $1000 apiece for advice on how to Out-source American jobs to cheap-cost-labor overseas labor markets. Protesters got wind of the conference and picketed with signs reading, "Be American. Buy American." Something to think about?...But inside the hotel, the signs celebrated Off-shore and Out-sourcing. Consulting firm Covance bragged that "We pioneered the transparent Off-shore Out-sourcing model." Executives attending the event learned the finer points of doing business in emerging labor markets such as Russia, the Philippines, and Vietnam. One seminar was intriguingly titled, "**Is**

Off-shore Sourcing Unpatriotic?" Something to think about, that seminar was closed to any news media, WHY? **The thing that's not being communicated at these conferences is that American multinational companies that are Out-sourcing are also essentially firing their customers.**

India can provide our software; China can provide our toys; Sri Lanka can make our clothes; Japan can make our cars. But at some point we have to ask, what will we Out-source? At what will Americans work? And for what kind of wages? No one in government, business, or academia has been able to answer those questions.

2

Americans right to Work?

I believe in the dignity of labor, whether with head or hand, that the world owes no man a living, but that it owes every man an opportunity to make a living.

—JOHN D. ROCKEFELLER

A good example of an American CEO in Crisis was Hewlett-Packard Chairwoman and CEO Carly Fiorina, who declared in 2004 that "No American has a God-given right to a job." My first reaction when I read her statement was, "You-just jumped off the bridge, Carly Fiorina, **a CEO challenging God?**." That first reaction has held up as a lasting impression. As much as I don't like what she said, I do give Fiorina credit for **straight-talk**, <u>and that is that American CEOs are in Crisis and are simply responding without proper option</u>. She didn't *cookie-glaze* her sentiments for public consumption, because she didn't have to. Years ago, Fiorina's bold statement, and its clear implications, would have fueled-a-tanker of labor protest and political controversy, but maybe "America" may be waking up to what is happening with its CEOs in Crisis. The HP CEO and Chairwoman was fired by her Board, February 8th, 2005, or did GOD disagree, you decide.

Working men and women in this country are becoming less part of the political equation or to be specific it is the who-likes-who contest. **Business and capital rule**. It's that simple. How has Corporate America reached such a higher power that there is seemingly no countervailing influence to its primary over public policy and international trade? The answers are complex and varying. Globalization and technology have transformed our industrial economy into one of services and knowledge-based enterprises because of market demands. Our population has more than doubled in the past forty years, and while we can proudly boast of being the most diverse society in the world, identity politics have superseded the corner-stone of fair trade. We have become a nation where affiliation with a political party and its ideology has become more important and easier than dealing intelligently with specific issues on a case-by-case basis. The result is that many times our political leaders don't adequately focus on the important social issues that are of national American common cause.

The truth is, Many of our elected officials, whether Republican or Democrat, have decided that whatever is **good for big business is good for America.** Never have government and big business been in a tighter embrace. It's the **"boomerang-era"** President Woodrow Wilson was hardly the shy, retiring brand of capitalist, but his statement was relatively mild compared to the FMR HP CEO and Chairwoman Carly Fiorina's declaration of ruthless capitalism. It makes you wonder, if Fiorina thinks there's no right to a job, what other rights would she have us surrender in order for her and other CEOs in Crisis to drive up quarterly profits and their companies' stock price? Would it make it less strenuous for our overstressed yet highly compensated American CEOs who are in Crisis, if we were to repeal OSHA and workmen's compensation? How about getting rid of those burdensome clean air and water laws? Do we really need those silly child labor laws? I wish I could tell you that Fiorina is part of a small minority in Corporate America, but she's not. Fiorina the FMR HP CEO and Chairwoman simply said out loud and straightforwardly what most American CEOs are in crisis and should do better but are thinking when they pursue short-term profits with regard for nothing but themselves and their investors. Their employees, the communities in which they work, and, yes, the nation all fall by the wayside. No matter what the pain to American workers. Quite simply though, the problem is that more and more American companies, and American CEOs in Crisis and even some **government agencies, are sending American jobs and technologies overseas purely to cut labor costs**. In the process, however, we are losing high quality jobs in this country by the thousands every month. Jobs that were once filled by American workers whether blue-collar factory workers or white-collar professionals-are now being performed by people in other countries for a fraction of the pay that American workers used to take home.

To put it bluntly, I don't think we're getting those jobs back. At least not until our business and government leaders decide to do something about it, which seems to be slowly taking place. American CEOs in crisis tend to not comprehend that Outsourcing threatens our economy, our jobs, and our way of life, or they choose not to comprehend or care. But there is help on the way in 2005…Getting many **American CEOs** can do better we have the technology and politicians to understand this is going to be tough, because they simply don't believe that anything or anyone should interfere with their views of the political economy. Irresistibly, some business leaders act wholly in their self-interest, freed by the Market of concern for their employees, their communities and broad obligations to our American society. And many of our elected officials in both parties choose not to annoy the Market. Allegiance and fidelity to free-trade, opposition-to-regulation, and unfettered-free-enterprise are the basic tenets of the true believers, whether politicians, American CEOs in Crisis, or academics. Cut-to-the-chase, if our corporate leaders had demonstrated greater success in global competition, I might be far more inclined to take some of their views more seriously. But as I see it, they are Out-sourcing jobs because they and their corporate enablers, consultants like **Accenture** and **McKinsey**, are simply fresh out of new ideas. And working men and women are paying the price.

It's been almost four years since the end of the 2001 recession. Despite strong growth, the American economy has only just begun to create jobs, and those jobs, in the main, aren't the high-paying, high-value jobs typically created in recovery from a recession? Our trade deficits and budget deficits are soaring, together amounting to a trillion dollars a year. Even with solid economic growth and outstanding corporate earnings, good jobs aren't being created at a rate in so far early 2005, sufficient to keep up with population growth.

The outstanding corporate profits are the result of higher productivity, and at least part of the credit for that improvement should go to the American worker. For the past several years, business has pushed fewer employees to work longer hours to produce more-and often without additional compensation. Since American companies began shedding jobs during the recent economic downturn, employees who remained behind are working more in order to avoid being the next American worker, person selected to be cut.

One American CEO in Crisis exclaimed: "Worker health problems, Worker safety, investor protection, product liability, national security of American technologies, consumer laws, and eliminate corporate tax obligations altogether...and while we're at it, let's repeal those unfriendly antitrust laws." There's no doubt the result would be sharply lower wages and higher profits..., but please someone yell out! the result would also be a plummeting standard of living and the shattering of the American dream...

The managements of many of our largest companies obviously don't share the American dream or they have already lived it, and the hell with everyone else, its time to move-on. Or they believe that because their companies are U.S. multinational corporations, they have less-or no-responsibility to preserve that dream. The American CEO in Crisis seems to think that their businesses are, first and foremost, international companies, not

American ones. Otherwise they couldn't routinely ignore the needs of their employees and their communities and Outsource their jobs to lower-paid workers in other countries.

The Out-sourcing of American jobs abroad is a relatively recent phenomenon in our history. But in the course of the past thirty years, we've lost millions upon millions of manufacturing jobs, and American CEOs, economists, and policy makers-Democrat and Republican have assured us that all this is the inevitable result of "postindustrial, modern economies, both advanced and developing, seeking comparative advantage, which will result in a higher standard of living for all of us...". It is worth noting, that our policy makers' assurances have largely been based on the research, study, and influence of powerful business lobbyists, who typically have been more than a little indifferent both to the welfare of the American economy-in which they themselves are based-and to the labor market, which also happens to be the principal component of what is by far the world's richest consumer market, the good old U.S.A. We are now witnessing the Out-sourcing of high-value jobs in IT (information technology), financial services, law, and engineering to low-cost labor markets all over the globe. Corporate CEOs in crisis and many private economists (called "private economists" because in most cases they are in the employment and payroll of private businesses, usually large multinational corporations) speak glibly about the blessings of higher productivity, the importance of efficiency, and the holy grail of global competitiveness. It's almost reached the point at which it all sounds like a mantra, at least to those of us who are not "true believers. Despite what American CEOs in crisis, Corporate America is suggesting, American workers are productive-in fact, the most productive in the world.

American workers aren't failing to compete with workers in any part of the global economy. The truth is, American workers aren't being asked to compete; U.S. multinationals are asking them to give up their standard of living and their quality of life, or else. Forrester Research estimates that $151.2 billion in wages will be shifted from the United States to lower wage countries by 2015. That includes about 3.4 million white-collar service jobs. Interestingly, the sector leading the way will be the IT information technology industry, which by the way represents America's National security technology industry. There's a cruel irony at work here: I think of the date and social security issues that are being told to Americans. No one batted an eye when we moved manufacturing jobs out of the country, because we were sure those jobs would be absorbed in the services sector-specifically, the information technology industry.

Some jobs are sent overseas routinely: back-office accounting and call-center work such as customer calling and customer-support. But over time, according to Forrester, even jobs that require higher skill sets will be sent to other countries. These include professional jobs in areas such as architecture, life sciences, law, and business management. Forrester thinks that roughly 550 of the 700 service job categories in the United States will be affected by Out-sourcing in the coming decade.

It's not just American corporations that are sending these jobs overseas.

Many state and local governments are following the pathetic example set by Corporate America. And the trend is expected to worsen, but in this year so far 2005 seems to be reversing in some states. A recent study by Input Research found that the market for state and local government information technology Out-sourcing will grow from $10 billion in 2003 to $23 billion in 2008. The problem now, however, is that some state and local governments are not simply Out-sourcing jobs to contractors that employ American workers. Several government agencies have actually begun to Out-source work to firms that utilize cheap-cost-labor, foreign labor.

Forty state governments are now Out-sourcing what were American jobs. The state of Indiana's Department of Workforce Development is responsible for helping out-of-work Indiana citizens find jobs. Ironically, the department awarded a $15 million contract to update its computers to the Bombay firm Tata.

The project would have provided employment for sixty-five workers coming from India on L-1 visas. Ironic, "*tata*" in English slang means goodbye, yes…The reason given for the move was the millions in tax dollars it would save the taxpayers of Indiana. But the taxpayers of Indiana, (by the way my wife is from Indiana) like most of us, would have preferred that their tax dollars be used to help those out-of-work Indiana residents find jobs. Only after a loud public outcry did the governor of Indiana cancel the contract.

That such a deal was even cut is, of course, the worst kind of shortsighted thinking. One reason for writing the American

CEOs can do better we have the technology is to help the thinking process of CEOs in crisis making decisions without option to American CEOs making better decisions. People who don't work don't pay taxes. And if American companies are paying a worker overseas to do a job, that foreign worker is not paying taxes in this country. Keeping tax dollars here will continue to be crucial as states struggle to repair their finances. The Center on Budget and Policy Priorities found that weak tax revenues will contribute to the state budgetary shortfalls that will persist through 2005. According to the study, states will have additional combined annual budgetary gaps of more than $40 billion in 2005, on top of the $78 billion already reported for 2004.

Unfortunately, it's not just big business and the government that are compromising future American prosperity by seeking the cheap-cost-labor foreign labor possible. Small and medium-sized businesses and professionals are also contracting out their call-center work, telemarketing, and design and engineering work. The odds are high that a radiologist in India read and analyzed your last X-ray for your doctor and local hospital. And now a number of HMOs, insurance companies, banks, and credit card companies are processing your personal medical and financial information overseas. **Of course, those countries don't have the same laws against the sharing and release of your personal information that you would enjoy had those records remained in the United States.** Those corporations Out-sourcing jobs to cheap-cost foreign labor-cost markets and Out-sourcing your medical and financial records are not only forfeiting American jobs and perhaps your privacy for short-term gain; they are also reducing tax revenues for local, state, and federal governments and adding to this country's trade deficit and current budget deficit. This has significant ramifications for our economy. Our trade deficit will continue to grow as we buy more from other countries than they buy from us, while our budget deficit proceeds on a downhill-ride as our government spends more money than it takes in. With the importation of a trillion dollars of foreign produced goods, we lose a trillion dollars of the U.S. consumer market. And we have no way to make it up, because there is no foreign market large enough to replace that trillion dollars. The result of the importation of foreign manufactured goods and the Out-sourceation of high value American jobs is to dampen job creation, further erode our manufacturing base, widen our trade deficit, and worsen our position as a debtor nation to the world. In economics, that isn't what they call a "happy result".

At least not for America. It's a very happy result for China, Japan, the EU, Canada, the Philippines, Ireland, India, and a host of other countries around the world. Altogether, our trade deficit over the years, which also represents our insatiable appetite for those foreign goods and imported oil, has put three trillion American dollars in the treasuries and business accounts of foreign countries. Its true, much of that money comes back as investment in our financial markets, but those trillions of dollars amount to America's IOUs to the world. The world, in other words, now has a rightful and lawful claim of more than three trillion dollars on American assets. And their claims to our assets will only rise as our deficits widen.

For all the talk about global competitiveness and being the most productive labor force in the world, U.S. multinationals just haven't been able to sell as many goods and services abroad as Americans want to buy. Not only are we buying most of our goods from other countries, we're also increasingly buying back our services from other countries. The high-value jobs that are being Out-sourceed to various countries around the world are not being sent overseas for the purpose of opening up these markets to U.S. products. Rather, those jobs are lost here, shipped there, and then that foreign labor works on the good or service for sale back to the United States. The result: We're Out-sourcing jobs overseas to create goods and services that are then provided to this Great American Marketplace. **I think maybe...I just got your attention**.

I am neither a total free-trader nor a total protectionist, but I do admit to being extremely parochial (I am an American) in my view of global trade. My first and principal concern is the well-being of this country, America and I'm sure it's yours as well. That is, unless you happen to be the American CEO in Crisis of a multinational corporation, or desire to be such, or you are a politician persuaded by powerful lobbying groups to overlook our national interest in favor of short-term profits for their clients, who see borders as occasional inconveniences. Business groups claiming that **Out-sourcing is good for the U.S. economy have simply gotten it half-right**. They claim that jobs lost to Out-sourcing are simply transferred to new and emerging industries-that the displaced worker ends up in a new and equivalent job. As an example, the Information Technology Association of America (**ITAA**), which represents many of the high-tech firms that have been at the forefront of sending jobs overseas, published a report in March 2004 that, "conclusively demonstrates that worldwide sourcing of computer software and services increases the number of U.S. jobs, improves real wages for American workers." The claim here appears to be that the more jobs we send away, the better off we all are. The fact of the matter is that the high-paying jobs lost in the recession are being replaced by work in lower paying industries. Doesn't matter if you're a software programmer, a lawyer, or a medical technician-if your job gets Out-sourced, chances are that your next job will not pay as well as your old one.

It's time to begin questioning the current demands on our workforce and to talk straight about what higher productivity really means to our standard of living and what Out-sourcing really means for job security and well-being of hardworking Americans as well as its national security. Embrace fresh thinking, and demonstrate real concern for a people in need of a far more effective policy. Corporate America must find a conscience and face the reality that life in this country America is about far more than competitiveness and productivity, and many American CEOs in Crisis can chose better options.

3

Working in the era of the Boomerang

The Out-sourcing of American jobs and technologies continues to be a conscious and concerted effort by company CEOs in Crisis and their consultants to save money, so much so that today the profit for the Out-sourced company is leaving and Out-sourcing companies are declining business, that is the Out-sourcer company is starting to lose money. HP is a corporation that has pushed its suppliers so hard that the suppliers are declining the work. In the rush to show Wall Street ever improving short-term profits, companies have slashed payrolls and wages until there is little left to slash. They've found the solution to this seemingly intractable problem by replacing the existing workforce with a newer, cheap-cost-labor, less reliable/quality version.

The corporations that have Out-sourced domestically for years, and the consulting firms paid to help them save money, took the concept to the next logical level: Out-source abroad.

Consulting firms like **Accenture and McKinsey & Company were early adapters and enablers of the strategy. McKinsey created detailed analyses of how much money, down to the penny, companies can save if they optioned for overseas labor instead of employing American workers.** And while consultants deny that the Out-sourcing of American jobs and technology is widespread, Out-sourcing revenue is the fastest growing part of their profits?

Businesses are started and run to make money...it's the essence of capitalism. But businesses also rely on their customers, employees, and suppliers, and that means there is also a responsibility to those stakeholders and not just to the investors. Despite their behavior, American CEOs in Crisis and their boards of directors are under no strict code of business management that insists that the profit margin is the only marker for a successful corporation. Listening to some CEOs, you might be forgiven for thinking that someone had absolved Corporate America of its social responsibilities. In the past few years, the concept of corporate responsibility in too many businesses seems to extend only to senior management. Everyone else is on their own. Time and time again in recent years, we've seen investors defrauded and employees laid off while CEO pay has skyrocketed. While wages in the United States have basically moved at a fraction pace for the past three decades, CEO compensation has risen astronomically, now amounting to about 400 times what the average employee earns. Obviously, Out-sourcing offers an opportunity for management to make that ratio even higher. Out-sourcing, or in 2005 a "fulfillment company", this is another name for Out-sourcing . The term has actually been used for the past several decades to describe the process of subcontracting services by the out-of-business Digital Equipment Corporation™ such as data processing or centralized corporate functions. In particular, companies who found that they were straining to keep up with technological advances were "Out-sourcing" the management and maintenance of their computer systems to companies better equipped to handle them, like IBM™ and EDS™. Out-sorcerss then ran the customer company's entire data processing division with their own staffs and resources, relieving the customer company of the need to build up core competencies it didn't possess, or to hire more staff with the necessary expertise. Out-sourcing also relieved the customer of the cost burdens of benefits and pensions. **That was Out-sourcing ten years ago**, and it also usually applied to staff or centralized departments such as back office accounting, or personnel and human resources.

Then came the term "Off-shoring," the building of plants and equipment overseas, often to provide facilities to bring back to the U.S. market products and services that were cheap-cost-labor overseas. This has been done since the early 1970s, when high-tech firms sent the manufacture of their semiconductors, computer keyboards, and printed circuit boards "offshore." American companies built or financed factories overseas because countries like Korea, Malaysia, Taiwan, Singapore, and eventually China were able to build large factories relatively inexpensively and staff them with cheap-cost-labor. Initially, many of those factories were built to create new capacity, because much of the primary manufacturing was still carried out by plants and facilities in the United States. And of course, Off-shoring bene-fited U.S. companies in that they were opening these interna-tional markets by building plants abroad, which allowed them to compete with the locals in selling competitively priced goods.

But, as American experts were sent to these overseas facilities to mentor their local managers and guide the foreign opera-tions, there was a considerable transfer of the expertise and knowledge from U.S. shores to the factories of the Pacific Rim. It wasn't long before the Asian managers were as good as their American counterparts. And the Out-sourcing trend was under-way, a trend that companies are capitalizing on today: With the transfer of expertise, knowledge, and skills, why not replace, wherever possible, expensive American labor with cheap-cost-labor foreign labor?

Several other factors were critical in the decision to develop offshore facilities. One, environmental regulations were all but nonexistent. This was especially helpful to companies that used or produced toxic chemicals in their manufacturing processes-which is to say, almost any company involved in producing computer components. Two, worker safety and health safe-guards were similarly nonexistent. Many of the factory workers in Asia (with the exception of Japan) during the 1970s and '80s labored under worse than sweatshop conditions. Those condi-tions still prevail in many countries, not only in Asia but also Latin America, although you tend to hear only about the ones producing celebrity clothing lines or athletic shoes. And third, these countries were essentially Third World economies, willing to provide financial incentives to almost any American company that would invest overseas.

These developments led to the broad Out-sourcing of American jobs and technologies. Today, Out-sourcing and Off-shoring fused together, and today in March of 2005 are termed: "Out-sourced Services, or a Fulfillment Company".

Show business and entertainment media were early adapters of the strategy. Popular animated cartoon shows like *The* Simpson's that were hand-drawn (not computer-generated) required a huge number of hours of inking and production to create a single episode. Producers of *The* Simpson's and other cartoons such as Rugrat's found that Korean companies had for years been doing this type of production for animated shows originating in Japan. The Koreans had built-in expertise, and, of course, their labor costs were minimal relative to the costs of paying Americans. Soon, the scripts and storyboards that were generated in Hollywood studios were shipped over to Korea for full animation and production. Other jobs, such as payroll and accounting, were among the first to be shipped overseas to take advantage of cheap-cost-labor.

After all, payroll isn't a specialized task, and the same data tends to carry over from month to month. Cheap-cost-labor foreign labor performing essential corporate functions was the hallmark of initial Out-sourcing.

And then Bangalore, India arose as the center of a huge amount of this work. This city of 5 million was teaming with well educated, skilled, English-speaking professionals. In the 1990s, Bangalore and other cities, such as **Bombay**, worked at a feverish pace to set up offices with high-speed tele communications lines that could communicate at a moment's notice with customers anywhere in the world. And one of the beautiful things about Bangalore, from a corporate perspective, was its time zone. Bangalore is on the other side of the world, and its twelve workable hours coincide with our nighttime. Work sent to Bangalore at the close of business in New York could be performed all night and be ready and waiting on those same New York desks when the offices reopened in the morning.

The Y2K bug scare propelled Out-sourcing ahead. It was feared the shortcuts made in computer programs over the past four decades would destroy the world's computers because there had been no provision for inputting the year "2000," and organizations all over the world rushed to have their codes upgraded or checked so that their computers wouldn't fail in the new millennium.

There was a lot of work to be done and a lot of software to be checked. Y2K compliance threatened to overwhelm nearly every organization that depended on computers. To handle the colossal task, **programmers in Bangalore were hired to help out. The software was sent to them over phone lines and the Internet, worked on, and then sent back-all while America slept.** In a matter of a couple of years, Bangalore found itself the high-tech capital of the Asian subcontinent. The Y2K meltdown was avoided-although not everyone is convinced it would have been inevitable, by the way-and the small enterprises in Bangalore were ready for more work. The employees of these companies were educated, spoke English, and had demonstrated their technical expertise. And they worked for a tenth of the pay that American programmers earned. Corporate America raised its eyebrows, focused on the bottom line, and signed on. Today more than 1,000 companies Out-source their business processes and technology maintenance needs to Bangalore.

The city has an estimated 160,000 programmers, and American companies are paying many of them.

The best programmers are living very well, on salaries of about **$12,000 to $21,000** a year. In the United States, that's just about the poverty threshold for a family of four. We've reached a point in Out-sourcing and Off-shoring where Corporate America is doing more than paying the salaries of Indian workers who handle data processing, or hiring a Malaysian company to balance the general ledger, or using a Taiwanese company to handle excess manufacturing needs. Companies are now Out-sourcing actual American jobs, jobs that can be identified and aren't just part of a general trend toward exploiting global consumer markets.

Why should America be so concerned about this now? After all, jobs and businesses have always moved-sometimes across town, sometimes across the state, sometimes across the country. The rise of multinational corporations has transformed what was once a competition between states-which had a positive effect on the national economy-into an unfair competition with low-cost labor in other countries. Of course, workers in North Carolina still pay taxes to the U.S. government, which ultimately benefits all of us. Cheap-cost-labor foreign labor neither pays U.S. taxes nor contributes to Social Security.

Technology has played the central role in Out-sourcing overseas. The so-called death-of-distance means that it now takes less time to move goods, services, capital, people, and information from one place to another. This phenomenon has been spurred on by a number of mechanical and technological innovations, beginning with the transcontinental railway and the use of steamships by immigrants. They moved people and jobs from Europe to the United States, and from the East Coast to the West Coast. In the 1950s and '60s, the national highway system and commercial air traffic cut distances, making the movement of people and products even easier.

Then came the high-tech drivers of the 1980s, including improved phone service, FedEx, and the fax machine. These allowed documents and data to be transferred in time that was measured in minutes or hours rather than days or weeks. But the most important driver of modern change has obviously been the Internet. The seemingly real-time transfer of data over the Internet, from files and film to audio and video, has removed almost every remaining barrier to doing business in real time with anyone else on the planet. With the high-speed Internet connection, it's arguably easier to have someone halfway around the world review a document by e-mail than to get up and walk down the hall to talk with another person in the same office. This "death-of-distance" has created an alternative network of workers around the world. That global labor pool has also created a disconnection between American companies and their American workers. A still small, but increasing, number of American workers telecommute or have flex-time; they aren't in the office from eight to five, as they were ten or twenty years ago. Contact between workers and management occurs more often via e-mail and telephone and less often in person. From management's perspective, then, what's the difference between an American worker telecommuting from his home in the next town over and an Indian worker telecommuting from the other side of the globe? The result is still the same, isn't it? Hardly.

The cost to the corporation is the biggest difference, and the American worker will always lose any global contest decided by the price of cheap-labor.

The central question is this: Should American CEOs in Crisis force workers to compete for their jobs-providing goods and services to the American market-with workers in countries like India and China who make a fraction of U.S. wages? I believe the answer is "absolutely not." As much as I admire what the Chinese and Indians are achieving, I'm not one of those who believe in "trade as aid." For most of the workers in those countries, the increase in the standard of living that they earn from an Out-sourced American job elevates them to the upper-middle-class of their societies. But the fact is, we're jeopardizing our middle-class if we continue this dangerous trend. I'd much prefer that American CEOs look to their obligations to American workers and phase-out Out-sourcing, instead of rationalizing what is simply a cost-cutting measure for cheap labor and conduct business in a fair, even playing field. And I'd certainly prefer that our government look to the risks of one-sided "free-trade" agreements that have resulted in a flood of imports into the United States. Incredibly, the federal government hasn't developed data about how these so-called free-trade agreements affect American companies and American workers yet. We do know we have more than a half-trillion-dollar trade deficit. And we know we have to borrow hundreds of billions of dollars to finance our consumption of those imports. Fourteen years ago Congress mandated economic as well as environmental impact statements on domestic policies but failed to extend the requirement for such research into foreign policy and international trade. In my humble opinion, Congress should do so, soon...

Corporations have overwhelmed governments in the borderless global economy. And corporate logos in many cases have more powerful symbolic importance than national flags. In part, that's because more than half of the 100 largest economies in the entire world are corporations. That's right, there are now more companies than countries on the list of the world's top 100 economies.

THE TOP 100 ECONOMIES:

Country/Corporation GDP/Out-sourcing sales ($mil)

1. **United States 8,708,870.0**

2. **Japan 4,395,083.0**

3. Germany 2,081,202.0

4. France 1,410,262.0

5. **United Kingdom 1,373,612.0**

6. Italy 1,149,958.0

7. **China 1,149,814.0**

8. Brazil 760,345.0

9. Canada 612,049.0

10. Spain 562,245.0

11. **Mexico 474,951.0**

12. **India 459,765.0**

13. **Korea, Rep. 406,940.0**

14. Australia 389,691.0

15. Netherlands 384,766.0

16. Russian Federation 375,345.0

17. Argentina 281,942.0

18. Switzerland 260,299.0

19. Belgium 245,706.0

20. Sweden 226,388.0

21. Austria 208,949.0

22. Turkey 188,374.0

23. **General Motors** 176,558.0

24. Denmark 174,363.0

25. **Wal-Mart** 166,809.0

26. **Exxon Mobil** 163,881.0

27. **Ford Motor** 162,558.0

28. **DaimlerChrysler** 159,985.7

29. Poland 154,146.0

30. Norway 145,449.0

31. Indonesia 140,964.0

32. South Africa 131,127.0

33. Saudi Arabia 128,892.0

34. Finland 126,130.0

35. Greece 123,934.0

36. Thailand 123,887.0

37. **Mitsui** 118,555.2

38. **Mitsubishi** 117,765.6

39. **Toyota Motor** 115,670.9

40. **General Electric** 111,630.0

41. **Itochu** 109,068.9

42. Portugal 107,716.0

43. **Royal Dutch/Shell** 105,366.0

44. Venezuela 103,918.0

45. Iran, Islamic Rep. 101,073.0

46. Israel 99,068.0

47. **Sumitomo** 95,701.6

48. **Nippon Tel. & Tel.** 93,591.7

49. Egypt, Arab Rep. 92,413.0

50. Marubeni 91,807.4

51. Colombia 88,596.0

52. AXA 87,645.7

53. IBM 87,548.0

54. Singapore 84,945.0

55. Ireland 84,861.0

56. BP Amoco 83,556.0

57. Citigroup 82,005.0

58. Volkswagen 80,072.7

59. Nippon *Life* Insurance 78,515.1

60. Philippines 75,350.0

61. **Siemens** 75,337.0

62. Malaysia 74,634.0

63. Allianz 74,178.2

64. **Hitachi** 71,858.5

65. Chile 71,092.0

66. **Matsushita Electric Ind.** 65,555.6

67. Nissho Iwai 65,393.2

68. **ING Group** 62,492.4

69. **AT&T** 62,391.0

70. **Philip Morris** 61,751.0

71. **Sony** 60,052.7

72. Pakistan 59,880.0

73. **Deutsche Bank** 58,585.1

74. **Boeing** 57,993.0

75. Peru 57,318.0

76. Czech Republic 56,379.0

77. **Dai-Ichi Mutual *Life* Ins.** 55,104.7

78. **Honda Motor** 54,773.5

79. Assicurazioni Generali 53,723.2

80. **Nissan Motor** 53,679.9

81. New Zealand 53,622.0

82. E.ON 52,227.7

83. **Toshiba** 51,634.9

84. **Bank of America** 51,392.0

85. **Fiat** 51,331.7

86. Nestle 49,694.1

87. SBC Communications 49,489.0

88. Credit Suisse 49,362.0

89. Hungary 48,355.0

90. **Hewlett-Packard 48,253.0**

91. Fujitsu 47,195.9

92. Algeria 47,015.0

93. Metro 46,663.6

94. Sumitomo Life Ins. 46,445.1

95. **Bangladesh 45,779.0**

96. Tokyo Electric Power 45,727.7

97. **Kroger 45,351.6**

98. Total Fina Elf 44,990.3

99. NEC 44,828.0

100. **State Farm Insurance 44,637.2**

(Fortune, July 31, 2000. GDP: World Bank, World *Development ment Report 2000, in 2004 these numbers on average w a 3% margin of error have increased almost 2x)*

4

America's risk of unfair free-trade

The budget should be balanced. Public debt should be reduced. The arrogance of officialdom should be tempered. And assistance to foreign lands should be curtailed lest Rome become bankrupt.

—CICERO

Incredibly, the proponents of Out-sourcing and free-trade will tell you that it's all a win-win proposition, remember win-win. It's been my experience that sometimes you should reach for your wallet when anyone says "win-win." Free-trade and Out-sourcing are no exceptions. There are winners and losers in our global economy, and the Yardstick for all to see and measure. The Commerce Department reports the U.S. trade deficit each month. Germany, Japan, Russia, Canada, Brazil, and China have enormous trade surpluses and are clear winners. Turkey, Australia, Israel, Egypt, and the United States run huge trade deficits and are clear losers. The United States is the biggest loser by far. We've been losing for so long that we're also the largest debtor nation in the world.

Free-trade implies that trading partners achieve balanced benefits for their economies. That isn't even close to being the case, unless you consider an annual half-trillion dollar trade deficit to be close. You have to wonder how our business and political leaders can keep a straight face when they describe our current trade policies as "**free-fair-balanced-trade**." It may be free to them, but the cost to America is exorbitant-and not only in dollar terms. The free-traders and their supporters say it's all just the cost of doing business, part of globalization, the global economy and part of the evolution of the international marketplace. Now our national policies are leading the United States toward diminished economic and political power, and unprecedented vulnerability to external forces that we may one day not be able to manage. And our government continues to negotiate trade deals without enunciating a clear vision of how our quality of life in this country America will be affected.

One of the effects is America's rising dependence on imports. For instance, we are reliant on the rest of the world for our energy needs. U.S. imports of petroleum products have increased by more than 200 percent since 1970, with goods from the Persian Gulf now representing almost one-fifth of the crude oil products we import. Moreover, net imports of petroleum are expected to grow from 55 percent of our total demand in 2001 to 68 percent of demand by 2025. A 1997 White House study found that improvements in the fuel efficiency of cars and trucks could reduce our oil use in 2030 by six million barrels per day. And one estimate from a pro-drilling group found that production from the Arctic National Wildlife Refuge could replace up to 70 percent of our imports from the Persian Gulf. But because our political parties view domestic production and conservation in purely partisan terms rather than in the national interest, we have done nothing to reduce our dependency on other nations to meet our energy requirements. Simply today March 15th, 2005 a gallon of premium gas costs $2.19, in Houston, Texas and it is premium costs that Americans watch, because regular grade gasoline is taughted as "not really a good grade of fuel to operate on long term". Our dependency on foreign resources extends well beyond energy. According to a study conducted by the Center for Labor Market Studies at Northeastern University, the United States is more dependent on immigration to meet its labor force requirements than at any time in the past eighty plus years. This dependency is principally the result of so many businesses being unwilling to pay a fair living wage to our American workforce to fill those jobs.

We should be worrying about the prospect of more jobs and more businesses being wiped out by cheap-cost foreign labor, and even more worried about those who blindly advocate free-trade for its own sake-well, actually, for the sake of powerful U.S. multinational corporations.

U.S. companies and multinational corporations operating in the United States pushed hard for the Free-trade Area of the Americas in 2003, arguing that it would open new markets for the United States' $10 trillion economy. But we'd heard this specious logic before-one decade and nearly one million jobs ago. Proponents of NAFTA declared that the 1994 pact would create 170,000 U.S. jobs annually.

Instead, at least 760,000 American jobs were lost as a direct result of NAFTA. The Economic Policy Institute found that about four-fifths of those were in the manufacturing sector. When high-wage manufacturing jobs are replaced with service sector jobs it pays at least 27 percent less, the downward pressure on the wages of Americans is accelerated and is continuing. Free-trade hasn't been entirely beneficial to our trading partners, either. NAFTA supporters predicted that Mexican workers would see increased wages, stemming the tide of Mexican migration. But Mexican manufacturing wages actually fell 26 percent between 1994 and 2000, and the number of Mexicans living in poverty today 2005 now includes more than two-thirds of the population. As a consequence, NAFTA has stimulated illegal migration to the United States. Eight million to twelve million illegal aliens reside here, and more than half of them have crossed our southern border in the past decade.

NAFTA transformed a relatively manageable trade deficit with our neighbors into a full-blown problem. While U.S. Outsources to Mexico and Canada have increased by 59 percent, imports have risen 97 percent. Read this again, While U.S. Out-sources to Mexico and Canada have increased by 59 percent, imports have risen 97 percent. Fair and balanced, you decide. As a result, the U.S. trade deficit with those two countries has ballooned from $10 billion in 1993 to $91 billion last year and it's only getting worse.

The creation of millions of jobs during the 1990s masked the true detriments of free-trade. But now that we can see the effects on our nation's workforce, economy, and quality of life. Here's what the modern application of free-trade really costs, **lets look at some history together:** In 1951 the average U.S. trade tariff was approximately 15 percent. By 1979 the average industrial tariff sank to 5.7 percent, and now our industrial tariff on foreign goods is just under 3 percent. As a result, the United States has become the world's greatest customer on credit, accumulating a trade deficit every year since 1976-the cumulative total of which is a staggering $3.5 trillion. And countries like China, Japan, Germany, Canada, and Mexico are the primary beneficiaries. **Wal-Mart** alone will import nearly $15 billion in goods this year from **China.** In fact, **Wal-Mart as a single company is China's fifth largest Out-source market in the world.** Remember when the marketing message of Wal-Mart was "**Made in America**"? **No more.** And it's not just Wal-Mart. Surveys show that **Americans can't buy American even if they want to.** The Economic Policy Institute estimates that 99 percent of our trade deficit comes from goods we now buy overseas because we no longer make them here. Eighty-nine percent of consumers who look for American-made

goods say they have a hard time finding them, and the reason for this is simple:

We've given away our manufacturing base through "free" trade. At least **85 percent of toys** sold in the United States are foreign-made, according to the Toy Industry Association. Ninety-eight percent of all clothing purchased in the United

States is now imported. **Is that because foreign workers are smarter or more productive or have a better education or work ethic? No**, it's because our principal trading partners have amazingly cheap-cost labor costs. For example, the average manufacturing wage in China is 73 cents per hour, while the average in America is $16. Pursuing free-trade policies that force the American worker to compete against third world workers with that kind of pay differential is patently unfair and absurd. It's actually surprising that we've lost only three million manufacturing jobs in the past three years. All for short-term profits for U.S. multinationals, and of course, all in the name of free-trade.

We are in desperate need of new thinking on trade, the fairness of current policies, and what kind of country we want our children to live in when we are gone. At the very least, we need to begin to pursue a national policy of balanced trade. It's time for all of us to realize that a purely ideological commitment to free-trade is as foolhardy as absolute protectionism.

There is no more glaring example of the folly of unrestricted trade than China. The United States ran an almost $126 billion goods deficit with China in 2004. The closest thing to a problem for China is the American demand that they abandon the peg of their currency, the yuan, to the dollar. (China pegs, or fixes, its currency to the dollar at a level of 8.29 yuan to one dollar. The result is that the yuan is very cheap right now, which keeps Chinese goods at extremely low costs in the international marketplace.)

The dollar peg isn't a problem for the Chinese; in fact, it further helps to keep their sales to the United States cheap-labor-costed. No, the problem is that the Chinese don't like anyone, and certainly not the United States, to criticize their economic policies. Not only is our trade deficit with China likely to set another record, but thousands of high-value American jobs continue to be lost to cheap-cost Chinese labor. No, the problems in the relationship are America's, right? By the way, China has again rebuffed the U.S. call to end the yuan-dollar peg. Premier Wen of China insisted that the rapid expansion of trade has benefited both countries. As you might expect, he suggests the solution is not to reduce Chinese imports but rather to increase U.S. Out-sources to China.

"We seek mutual benefits and win-win results. We should look at the larger picture and larger interests of our trade for each country." And when we do look at the larger picture, and consider U.S. interests, we still have a crushing trade deficit with China, with no prospect of a fair and balanced agreement in the near future.

In fact, China surpassed the United States as the most popular destination for foreign direct investment last year. And ten of China's top forty Out-sorcererss are U.S.-based companies, such as **Motorola**. As I said, the problems Premier Wen acknowledged are American problems.

The relationship with China is emblematic of our relationship with much of Asia and Europe. Almost half the U.S. treasury bonds are now owned in Asia, **buy bonds, right?** Not only have we become dependent on Asia and Europe for goods and services-and apparently cheap-labor-costs but we are also now dependent on them for the capital to finance our purchases of their imports. It's hard to imagine how we could construct more destructive trade policies. Whether it is the importation of petroleum or clothing and food, the Out-sourceation of jobs and manufacturing, or the foreign ownership of securities and bonds, America's dependency on the rest of the world has risen to dangerous levels. Successive administrations of Democrats and Republicans alike in Washington have been either unable or unwilling to confront America's rising vulnerability to external forces until just recently.

5

Abraham Lincoln, At what cost for free-trade

I see in the near future a crisis approaching that unnerves me and causes me to tremble for the safety of my country. As a result of the war, corporations have been enthroned and an era of corruption in high places will follow, and the money power of the country will endeavor to prolong its reign by working upon the prejudices of the people until all wealth is aggregated in a few hands and the Republic is destroyed.

—ABRAHAM LINCOLN

Cold *Mountain,* the best-selling novel about the Civil War, was turned into a feature film in 2003. The film was nominated for an Oscar for its cinematography and won praise for its gritty and bone chilling depiction of America during the waning days of the Civil War. But **Cold** *Mountain* wasn't filmed in America. **It was filmed in Romania.** The reason for filming in Eastern Europe was to save money for the film's producer, Miramax. The film had a budget of $90 million, but Miramax received more than $10 million of that budget back in the form of tax incentives from foreign governments for shooting overseas. **Gangs of New York** wasn't filmed in New York, either; **it was filmed in Italy.** The TV movie *The Reagans* **was filmed in Toronto**, and *The Rudy Giuliani Story* **was shot in Montreal.** Classic American stories, with nary an American production in sight.

In 2003, of the eighty-nine American movies made for television, only six were made in this country. We've been hearing and reading about filming done in other countries because of the costs of making movies in the United States. But it's now gotten to the point where the U.S. market share of movie production has **fallen** 22 **percent** in the past seven years. Benefiting from that drop are countries including Canada, Australia, and New Zealand as well as Eastern Europe. According to the Film and Television Action Committee, that translates to about 21,000 lost jobs per year. This is hardly a reason to shout, "Hooray for Hollywood, you think?"

But film production is only one of a mind-boggling number of businesses that are cutting costs by going to other countries. It's one thing to think about acting and production jobs being sent to Canada or Romania, but what about engineering, medical technicians? Lawyers? Architects? These are high-paying professional jobs that we've always thought could never get sent overseas. **We couldn't have been more wrong. Not only can white-collar jobs get outsourced, they already are.**

We're accustomed, and almost immune, to the fact that manufacturing jobs have been disappearing in this country for

decades. We've all heard the upside, too: how blue-collar workers are getting training and finding higher-paying professional-
and white-collar-jobs after losing their factory jobs. That sce-
nario doesn't seem quite so optimistic when you realize that the
white-collar jobs are heading overseas as well. If blue-collar and
manufacturing jobs lead to white-collar jobs, where do white-
collar jobs lead? Right now, they lead to low-paying wages in
another country. The truth is that we can't afford to lose either
our manufacturing base or our professional jobs, American
CEOs need to know this fact. If that happens, we will be in a
position where we as Americans, that includes American CEOs
that are making these decisions don't make or develop anything
that we buy-which raises concerns about our level of dependence on other countries. We've seen how nasty things can get
when the producers of oil decide to withhold their products
from our country, look at the gas prices at the pump. Imagine if
the manufacturers of our everyday items decide it's time to hold
back on providing those goods to us, regardless of the cost.

Even though there are a huge number of people employed in
America's service sector, we can't afford to allow jobs in those
businesses to start eroding. Service sector jobs account for more
than 60 percent of the employment in the United States, compared to *14* percent for manufacturing.

There are few places in the United States as emblematic of
our service sector success as California's Silicon Valley, Colo-
rado, and Texas, (yes, Texas does more than oil and ride horses)
home to many of our biggest high-tech firms and some of our
most skilled technology workers. But right now all are under the

same kind of attack to which our industrial centers have been subject. Don't take my word for it. Here's a headline from *The Times of India,* dated January 6, *2004:* SILICON VALLEY PALLS TO BANGALORE.

The newspaper boasted that Bangalore now has 150,000 information technology engineers, which it says *is 20,000* more than are currently employed in Silicon Valley. And when you consider how many American companies are using services based in Bangalore, that headline may not be too far off the mark. India is only one of the many countries benefiting from the Out-sourcing of American jobs. But it has also been one of the most aggressive in pursuing professional-level jobs, from medical technicians to software programmers. American companies have been all too happy to answer India's siren call of educated English-speakers willing to work at some of the world's lowest wages ever heard of. For example, General Electric's Capital International Services (CIS) was one of the pioneers in shipping domestic operations to India. In fact, it bills itself as the "largest shared-services environment in India." CIS now has four centers in that country, employing more than 13,000 workers, and claims to have realized savings of more than $300 million a year. The people there write software; they review invoices and insurance claims; they do market analysis. CIS also offers its services to other American companies looking for Out-sourced resources. Let's look at several different job categories at the professional level, like those that Capital International Services offers, and describe what's really happening. Let's start with software programmers. There are programmers all over the world, but the Indian Institutes of Technology (known as **IIT' s**) are turning out thousands of these pro-grammers a year. They are men and women who are well edu-cated, speak impeccable English, and are thrilled to make $10,000 a year. Indians talents are not in manufacturing-it lags far behind other Asian countries in that respect-but it is no slouch in the services sector. That makes India well positioned to siphon off some of our highest-paying and most desirable jobs. The high-tech industry is especially susceptible to Out-sourcing. With the exception of hardware, just about every aspect of the computer business can be Out-sourced. Systems software can be coded and debugged, applications can be tested and updated, and Customer Service's can be handled anywhere a company wants to set up the necessary transmission lines. The high-tech industry, in setting up an infrastructure for transmit-ting its products, not only internally but also to its customers (many of whom now download their software directly from the vendors instead of buying boxed software and CDs), has also created a means for shipping its own jobs overseas. Out-sourc-ing is rampant in the high-tech industry, not only because of how easy it is but because of the desire to cut margins in a cut-throat business.

As an example, **IBM**, once the biggest and most respected name in high tech, is now one of the biggest proponents of Out-sourcing. The company said in early 2004 that it would add an estimated 15,000 new employees during the year. At first it appeared to be a sign that at least one company was try-ing to fight the jobless recovery. **Unfortunately**, further investigation showed that more than two-thirds of IBM's new jobs would be based outside America. Only 4,500 of those jobs were slated for the United States.

Then IBM also said it would be shifting 3,000 existing jobs out of the United States. That means a net gain of only 1,500 jobs in America, with nearly 15,000 jobs going overseas, more than 10,000 of them newly created. **Asked about why** this was being done, an IBM **spokesman said, "We're doing** it because there's growth in those areas…this is pretty good news for us and the industry."

The **Wall Street** *journal* reported that **IBM** calculated the cost of an American programmer at $156 an hour, including pay and benefits. A programmer based in China was calculated to cost the company $12.50 an hour. Citing internal IBM memos, the *journal* said that IBM advised managers who were told to break the news about overseas jobs never to use the word "On-shore" or "Off-shore."

IBM called the *journal* reports inaccurate, but I found them to be bone chilling. Those internal documents said it would be the job of IBM's human resources and communications people to sanitize the discussions of any moves Off-shore, so that the process would never be portrayed as a movement to cut costs or to Out-source American jobs.

There are few companies as influential in this country as IBM. It is one that many consider to be both a thought leader and a leader in corporate behavior. Smaller companies around this country look to IBM for guidance in managing personnel and managing their businesses. So this kind of behavior goes beyond just IBM. **SAS Institute**, long known as one of the best companies to work for in the United States, and one of the largest privately held software firms, **is now an Out-sorcerers**, so perhaps it will *become one* of the best companies to work for in India. Founder Jim Goodnight admits to being perplexed by the issue, but has managed to convince himself that it's more important for his company to act globally than locally. Goodnight told CIO magazine how corporate American CEOs are managing to rationalize the process: "We are perplexed about what extent we should expand our operations in India.

We've got about sixty people there now. With the price and the quality of the people, we're thinking, 'We really ought to do more of this." But there's our American flag, country and American CEO who made that decision, not the American government. We've lost our manufacturing jobs overseas; we've lost textiles; North Carolina is losing its furniture industry. I keep preaching, and to my own family that we've got to train our children to be knowledge workers. But guess what? That's what they're doing in India, too. And the **Chinese** are picking up on that as well-not only are they doing all the manufacturing, *they're also* getting into **IT**. So it's going to be a major decision over the next few years for every company how much IT should be overseas. We've already *seen* the migration of call-*centers*. I think it's (Off-shore, Out-sourcing of IT) a concern, but I don't know what we can do about it, maybe our American CEOs have the answer. This issue has been bothering me a great deal-about whether we should put more resources into our Indian operations or not, it's very perplexing. Then I was reminded

that SAS is a global company. We're not just an American company, and we should put resources anywhere on the globe where
it makes sense. I'm slowly coming around to the idea that we
really might need to put more there (India]) and less in the U.S.
By the way, SAS is headquartered in Cary, North Carolina,
U.S.A, I think that's still America. Goodnight has the reputa-
tion of being one of the most generous employers in technology, so when he has to struggle not only with Out-sourcing
American jobs to cheap-cost labor markets, but also with
whether his company is American or global, we all need to take
a step back, take a deep breath, and begin to think. Really think
(**American CEOs** can do better we have the technology) about
who we are and what this country is all about. The high-tech
Off-shore exodus continues. Not so long ago, Bill Gates went to
India and promised to put $400 million of Microsoft's invest-
ment dollars into that country Microsoft's single biggest investment outside the United States. One hundred million of those
dollars will go to a development center that will employ 500
people, another $20 million to accelerating computer literacy in
India, and the biggest chunk-$280 million-to development of,
and training in, Microsoft technologies. *The Times of India*
reported that Microsoft has contracts with more than 3,000
Indian companies, which employ some 250,000 developers.
Those companies are developing products based on Microsoft
technologies, and the paper estimates that work on Microsoft
products constitutes nearly a quarter of the $8 billion worth of
Out-sourced work done in India. **Intel**, the world's largest
maker of computer chips, claims that since 70 percent of its

business comes from outside the United States, it's natural for the company to set up overseas operations. It's "just following its customers," **according to CEO Craig Barrett**. Addressing a crowd at an industry event, the Gartner Symposium IT-expo, Barrett was quick to blame the United States educational system and burdensome U.S. accounting and tax laws for Out-sourcing, indicating that companies were being forced to go overseas simply in order to protect their bottom lines. Yet his predecessor, **Mr. Andy Grove**, is not so sanguine. In fact, Grove has called for the government to help effect a balance between allowing businesses to provide shareholder value and helping them keep American workers employed. These contrasting views from the leader and former leader of Intel are all the more remarkable because it's a company that had to be saved from foreign competition in the 1980s, and a company that won a U.S. tax court ruling that allowed it to treat the sale of U.S. made microchips as income from its Japanese operations, which meant that it paid no U.S. taxes on those products. However, Japan treats those same profits as American-generated and thus requires no tax, either. Intel ended up not having to pay tax on these profits-at all. **Ross Perot** famously warned us about that "**sucking sound from the south**" as he opposed the creation of NAFTA. But the very companies he founded are Out-sorcererss. **Perot Systems is an IBM competitor** and a huge proponent of sending jobs overseas. Its plans for 2004 included the addition of more than 3,000 call-center and bill-processing jobs in India. The company also said it was creating two new facilities in that country during the year, which amounts to an investment of tens of millions of dollars. Downplaying the negatives, Perot said that this represented the company's purchase of Indian firms that already do Out-sourcing work. Despite the spin, Perot now has a substantial Indian operation involving thousands of employees, although Perot Systems was quoted as saying it had sent fewer than fifty jobs overseas. Perot Systems is now engaged in the kind of Out-sourcing that results in the Out-sourcing of American jobs. **Ross Perot owns 30 percent of Perot Systems.** He also founded EDS and was one of the first to bring the Out-sourcing of jobs to other countries to the national spotlight. Perot's warning about jobs going to Mexico was prophetic, of course, and hardly anyone thought he would be guilty of understatement. And no one at the time would have guessed that those jobs would also be heading in droves to India, the Philippines, Romania, Ireland, Poland, and various other quarters. And who would have guessed that Ross's company would be contributing to the problem? The number of high-tech firms that Out-source to India reads like a who's-who of the high-tech industry: **Apple, Computer Associates, Dell, Hewlett-Packard, Oracle, and Sun,** to name just a few. Executives from some of these companies attended the 2004 Reuters Technology, Media and Telecommunications Summit in New York and said they will create more jobs in countries such as India and China than they will in the United States. I guess that shouldn't be a big surprise to anyone, but last year U.S. technology employment dropped to its lowest level since 1998. And, as *The Times of India* reminds us, **technology companies outside the United States of American continue to BOOM!** While

hundreds of high-tech firms in the United States are Out-sourcing, the trend goes well beyond the high-tech industry. **Medicine**, that most personal of professions, is already Out-sourcing.
As health care costs increase, hospitals face the same pressures
that our factories face: the need to reduce the cost of operations.
Even in hospitals the search for the lowest-cost providers and
suppliers invariably results in Out-sourcing. Many of the
administrative aspects of health care, and certainly those involving accounting, have already made their way to countries like
India. Everything from creating invoices for patient treatment
and the processing of insurance claims to bill collection is routinely handled by Indian firms. Responding to concerns about
health care Out-sourcing, many hospitals shrug it off because it
doesn't involve actual patient contact or care. But Out-sourcing
is now part of the relationship between doctors and patients, a
relationship held to the highest standards of privacy. Medical
records and patient diagnoses, both real-time and recorded, are
sent over communications lines to India. There, transcribers
type out the doctor's words and send them back to the U.S.
hospital. They can then be printed out as documents and
inserted into the patient's medical file, all by the time the doctor
begins his next set of rounds. Massachusetts General Hospital,
one of the country's most prestigious medical institutions,
ignited a hellfire when it was learned that the hospital was sending X-rays and MRI scans to India for examination. The reading and interpretation of these images is the purview of
radiology, a medical specialty that has some **30,000 qualified**
members in the United States.

Apparently, hospitals think there are not enough of them or that they're overpaid. Radiologists, who routinely make upward of $250,000, are finding that Indian specialists are willing to do their jobs, in the middle of the night, at a tenth of the cost. Mass General, a **Harvard hospital** often referred to as "**Man's Greatest Hospital**," is only one of the many American hospitals **Out-sourcing pieces of patient care**. These hospitals and many doctors claim that it takes too long to get radiology data back, because radiologists don't or won't work nights, and that there aren't enough of them to call on as needed. The American College of Radiology backs this up by saying that demand far exceeds the number of qualified radiologists currently produced by med schools.

Technicians in India aren't legally allowed to perform diagnoses on U.S. patients, they'd have to be licensed here, but they help sort through data, provide interpretation, write preliminary reports, and turn two-dimensional images into more easily readable 3-D images. Because of the time difference in India, they provide after-hours services during their day, which coincides with nighttime hours here.

Even though **Medicare doesn't pay for work done outside the United States, the hospitals have found a way around that**. After getting the preliminary data back during the first hours of daylight, a licensed U.S. radiologist reviews the work and signs off on it. At that point it's all legit because an American doctor has signed his or her name to it. Medicare soon gets the bill. There are a huge number of concerns here, not the least of which is, **who is helping your doctor or hospital make**

decisions about your health and your treatment? Also, medical care is about as personal as professional contact gets, so it's of grave concern when you think that your records are being sent overseas to be handled by technicians or doctors **who are not licensed-and not even liable-in the United States**. Yet radiology is only one part of medicine vulnerable to Out-sourcing. The reading of other documents, such as **EKGs** and **EEGs**, is an obvious next step. So is the analysis of tissue samples, which can now be digitized and read by pathologists. How about assigning medication based on the review of these and other medical analyses and diagnoses? That may not be too far behind. And as doctors and patients begin to embrace remote monitoring of everything from vital signs to pacemakers, who's to say that such monitoring can't be done overseas? **The privacy issues are significant.**

Few countries have the same laws the United States has that protect patients' rights and doctor-patient confidentiality. How do you prosecute someone in India who might choose to disseminate information about patients? Or use it for their own gain? If that sounds a little too far-fetched, then you should know that it's already happened. **In 2003, the University of California, San Francisco Medical Center was subcontracting the transcription of doctors' dictation and various other medical records. The subcontractor Out-sourced the work to Pakistan**. There, an aggrieved Pakistani transcriber, claiming she had not been properly compensated, threatened to publicize the medical records she was working on. She sent an e-mail to UCSF demanding payment, or else. The blackmail worked, and the woman was paid. **The vulnerability is real to Americans**, and there's absolutely no way for American rights to be protected. But in an interesting twist, the **legal profession** is also at risk of **Out-sourcing**. And the reason is the same as everywhere else: **to cut costs**. Market research firm Forrester Research predicts that in the **next eleven years nearly 8 percent of law industry jobs will shift to low-cost countries**. Paralegal work and work done by junior lawyers is particularly vulnerable to Out-sourcing. Large legal firms, who pay young associates high salaries for doing lots of entry-level work, are looking for ways to cut costs. That can be done by shipping those jobs overseas. The first wave that's headed Off-shore is those jobs that can be commoditized. Large companies such as General Electric and BorgWarner are sending out their corporate legal work, such as research, because it costs less than giving it to domestic legal professionals. The concern is that the more work that is sent Off-shore to contract professionals in places like **India**, the less opportunity there will be for young lawyers here to get proper training. As with the medical profession, legal departments and law firms will probably send out the work normally done by paralegals, interns, and junior associates-certainly they wouldn't send out the work of highly paid partners. But one has to ask where less senior members of the staff will get their training if their work is being done on the other side of the world. These people, who often prepare drafts and do research, could be rendered unnecessary since senior partners usually look over these documents anyway. Their ability to do grunt work may thus become irrelevant if senior partners can save money by Out-sourcing it. These junior law professionals, such as paralegals, don't approve legal documents, so the law profession says there will be no impact on the final quality of legal work. They state that any work done overseas and used here must be approved by an American lawyer, who is then responsible for its contents. Having Indian legal professionals put it together is just a nice way to save time and money for these attorneys. To help make it even easier, some Indian firms are employing American lawyers to oversee their output so that it passes muster before it even gets shipped back to the United States.

Legal research and publishing have already discovered the cost-cutting benefits. So what's next? A lot of people would argue, and I would be one of them, that we don't need so many lawyers in this country. But we do need some, and we do need good ones. What happens when the first tier of entry to the legal profession gets closed off and shipped overseas? Will college graduates still be willing to invest the years of effort and the many thousands of dollars it takes to get a law degree? If they see legal jobs Out-sourced, will they determine that they have little to gain in an industry that puts less and less value on their knowledge and skills? The way things are going, it doesn't seem that we'll have to wait very long to find out. There is, of course, another load-a-bar of white-collar America that is taking a shine to Out-sourcing: the financial services industry. **JP Morgan, Morgan Stanley, and Goldman Sachs** all have operations in India, where research is turned out by financial analysts while Wall Street folks chill. The analysis is on their desks before the market opens in the United States. American Express has a center in Delhi running an international call-center and processing credit card transactions. Number of employees: 2,000. E-Serve, a division of Citigroup, has workers in Bombay and Chennai. Number of employees: 3,000.

This is just the beginning for Wall Street, "A. Kearney predicts that 500,000 financial services jobs will go offshore by 2008". I think that's a conservative estimate. One of the complaints I've heard from people is that when they call a financial services company or a technical support line, they find themselves talking to someone in India or another country. Yet the people on the other end identify themselves as Tom or Joan or John or Susan. Obviously, these are fake names employed for the reassurance of the American customer, who often has to struggle to understand what "Tom" or "Susan" is saying. Yet there is perhaps no other area of business that has been Outsourced so widely as call centers, and it is the subject of the most complaints from our viewers. Most of us have talked with call-centers when we call an airline for a reservation or check on our credit card balance or need help figuring out why our computer software won't work. **And more and more, these calls are going straight to India.** The country has the largest English-speaking population after the United States, and it even has schools that teach native Indians to speak with American regional dialects, obviously with varying degrees of success. **Indian call-centers started in the early 1990s**, due in large part to the efforts of **one man, Raman Roy. As an executive working with American Express** and later GE Capital, Roy spearheaded the creation of India-based business processing centers for American multinationals. Building a telecommunications infrastructure and taking full advantage of cheap-cost labor, he was able to save Amex and GE millions of dollars in cheap-labor-costs in a few short years. Spurred on by his success with both companies, he ventured out on his own and founded the company that has become Wipro Spectramind, today considered the dominant player in Indian Out-sourcing, with revenues of more than a billion dollars a year. The success of Wipro, Infosys, and other Indian technology companies is indisputable, and the most recent projections of Indian technology-sector growth are nearing $30 billion within the next few years. Entrepreneurial, and fully exploiting its low-wage advantage, the Indian technology sector is poised for continued global success. The fact remains that much of that success will be built on the transfer of jobs and knowledge from the U.S. marketplace. No one should blame the Indians for that transfer. The blame rests squarely with Corporate **American CEOs** that can do better we have the technology and our elected officials, who either support Out-sourcing or ignore its impact on our workers and our economy.

6

The Out-sorcerers

The Un-truths of Out-sourcing and Free-trade, All truth passes through three stages. First, it is ridiculed. Second, it is violently opposed, and denied. Third, it is accepted as being self-evident, validated and becomes policy.

—WAYNE HOLOVACS

Lets learn about Mr. Gregory Mankiw. He is a tall, handsome, bi-spectacled, bow-tied, low-keyed kind of a guy who looks the part of a former Harvard professor of economics, of which he is. Mr. Mankiw has written a number of popular economics type textbooks. He's also the chairman of the President's Council of Economic Advisers, and along with the president's economics adviser, Stephen Friedman, he has the greatest access to President George W. Bush on economic policy. Mr. Mankiw, however, chose again early this year to publicly support the shipment of American jobs to cheap-cost-labor overseas labor markets. He caused a brief out-cry in Congress, and even the always loyal Speaker of the House, Congressman Dennis Hastert, was moved to separate himself from Mr. Mankiw's statement. Mr. Mankiw said, "Out-sourcing is just a new way of doing international trade (and he is correct, *almost*). We are very used to goods being produced abroad and being shipped here on ships or planes. What we're not used to is services being produced abroad and being sent here over the Internet or telephone wires…I think Out-sourcing is a growing phenomenon, but it's something that we should realize is probably a plus for the economy in the long run."

Well…A number of people on Capitol Hill thought Mr. Mankiw should have resigned, but I disagreed. He should have been fired. Not merely because I obviously disagree with him, but because Mr. Mankiw's statement raised the administration's support of overseas Out-sourcing to a declaration of government policy. Now, maybe I'm being somewhat of a "girlyman" about the matter, but I just happen to believe that our government should be on the side of American working men and women, not aiding and abetting the destruction of the American job market by supporting a business practice that even Mr. Mankiw said could "probably be a plus for the economy in the long run." Probably? It could also be a probable negative without the proper fair and balanced process. It certainly isn't if you're one of the hundreds of thousands who've lost their jobs to Out-sourcing. When he added a further **qualifier to his support** by saying "in the long run," Mr. Mankiw kept his credentials as an economist in good standing. How long is the long run? How many jobs do we have to lose to Out-sourcing to determine whether it really is a "plus," or a definite negative? Mr. Mankiw spoke for the administration in his early support of Out-sourcing, and since then the President George W. Bush's economic team has taken its advocacy of free-trade at any price to new heights. The White House is not only making statements like "Out-sourcing is good for the American worker", but seems to forget that without a fair and balanced process the White House is Only half right, but is defending its free-trade policies by insisting that all of us who are concerned about chronic, bulging trade deficits and the Out-sourcing of American jobs are "ignorant". Candidly, I don't know anyone who has advocated any policy that could be honestly described as economic isolationism. And neither does the Bush administration. At a time when we should be having an honest, open dialogue. about the impact of overseas Out-sourcing and free, and balanced trade on American workers, the administration has chosen to semi-ignore the national cost of a half-trillion-dollar trade deficit, the huge quantities of foreign capital that we are now dependent on, and the emergence of a national policy that puts our working men and women, sons and daughters in direct competition for employment with a third world labor force that will work for cheap-foreign labor costs than Americans. There are a lot of misconceptions to address when we finally do begin that dialogue, and a lot of Un-truths to dispel.

Un-truth No. 1: Out-sourcing American jobs is good for our economy.

Even the chairman of the President's Council of Economic Advisers couldn't go beyond saying Out-sourcing is "probably" a plus for our economy, "in the long run." The problem is, there's no empirical evidence to support that position. We do know that workers who have lost their jobs to overseas Out-sourcing are finding new jobs that pay only about 80 percent of their original wages, if they are lucky. And we do know that there are tremendous costs to the government to provide unemployment benefits and retrain these laid off for those who are fortunate to receive this benefit.

Un-truth No. 2: Out-sourcing has improved productivity growth and the creation of high-value jobs. Our gains in productivity have resulted from (**1**) improvements in business processes and operations as a result of the application of new technology, (**2**) employees who are lucky enough to have had jobs for the past several years and are working longer hours for basically static compensation, and (**3**) moving production and shipping American jobs overseas to provide goods and services to the U.S. market.

As for creation of high-value jobs, the numbers speak for themselves, and they are not encouraging. When the Bureau of Labor Statistics released its ten-year projections for American job growth in February 2004, seven of the ten biggest areas of job growth were in menial or low paying service jobs.

Here's the BLS projection:

1. Waiters and waitresses

2. Janitors and cleaners

3. Food preparation

4. Nursing aides, orderlies, and attendants

5. Cashiers

6. Customer service representatives workers. Out-sourcing may be good for the profits of U.S. multi-nationals, but that isn't really the issue, is it?

7. Retail salespersons

8. Registered nurses

9. General and operational managers

10. Postsecondary teachers

[Only three of these job categories require a college degree. The rest rely on on-the-job training. These jobs of the future hardly qualify as high value, but are respectable jobs.]

Un-truth No. 3: Out-sourcing is simply a part of free-trade, and classical economists like Adam Smith and David Ricardo would have loved it. Adam Smith believed that free-trade allowed countries to concentrate their production on goods in which they had a natural advantage, and to acquire through trade other goods better produced by other countries. David Ricardo developed the concept of comparative advantage, which held that nations can benefit from free-trade by concentrating their production on goods they can produce most efficiently, acquiring through trade other goods that permit them to concentrate on their comparative advantage and thereby enlarge their economy. **Smith and Ricardo did not envision** a trade relationship in which there wasn't mutuality of benefit, that is, fairness and balance. Both economists assumed that national economies would act with a clear understanding of national self-interest. I doubt that either Smith or Ricardo would be pleased to find their free-trade theories being used to support the transfer of factors of production from developed nations to third world nations, to take advantage of all but limitless supplies of cheap-cost-labor foreign labor. They also could not have imagined that one nation would effectively risk bankrupting itself by transferring its comparative advantage of knowledge base, expertise, and capital to its trading partners, and then ship its jobs overseas as well. Our current trade policies aren't laissez-faire but rather 'Vest la vie." Remember America is at War with terrorism…!

Un-truth No. 4: Our economy and consumers are strong enough to run large chronic deficits, and historically a trade surplus is a sign of a weakening economy. This bizarre assertion was made by Congressman David Dreier-one of many he's made in trying to defend free-trade agreements. The Republican congressman from California is the personification of the free-trade-at-any-cost philosophy.

The congressman is partially correct, to the extent that a trade surplus might occur when an economy weakens or goes into recession, and the purchase of imports declines. But the reality is that with our chronic trade deficits we are approaching $4 trillion in accumulated trade-debt and must borrow foreign capital to buy foreign goods. As a result, our massive chronic trade deficits are clear evidence that our economy is not producing enough goods for domestic consumption and not producing enough goods that the world wants to buy or can afford. If that's not weakness, I don't know what is.

Un-truth No. 5: The only alternative to free-trade is protectionism or "economic isolationism." The free-traders insisting that there is only free-trade, as currently practiced, or no trade. But between the two extremes of free-trade and isolationism are a wide range of policy choices: In the center of the policy spectrum there is balanced trade. But many Washington and Corporate **America CEOs** that can do better are opposed to balanced trade because it would mean a new direction in policy, a larger and more active role for our government, and an end to carte blanche for corporations in international trade. The real alternative to what we continue to permit Washington and Corporate American CEOs to call "free-trade" in which we negotiate trade agreements that are reciprocal in benefit-unlike the World Trade Organization or trade agreements like **NAFTA**. We have ten years' experience with the **WTO**, and we have eleven years' experience with NAFTA. That experience shows that free-trade is not working for the United States. When the United States is carrying a half-trillion-dollar trade deficit, it's clearly not benefiting us. Many of our biggest trading partners, **notably China**, **are engaging in obstructed trade**, yet our leaders keep insisting that it's free and fair. They state that this is the only way it can work, or else we become protectionist. Well, the Chinese are protectionists, the Japanese are, and so is much of the EU. And they all have trade surpluses. Why should the United States of America not be able to achieve a surplus as well, or at least balanced trade?

Un-truth No. 6: Job retraining is the way to deal with Out-sourcing. Whenever industries and jobs have left our shores, we've retrained the workers for better jobs. That'll happen this time.

Mr. James Glassman, columnist for the *Washington* Post and an American Enterprise Institute fellow, answered this one just fine. When asked "**what we would be retraining workers for, Glassman said, "One of the things about a dynamic economy is, we don't know what the jobs are.**" And that's the point. When you're Out-sourcing jobs that are at or near the top of what we consider professional careers, where is the next step up? How do you tell engineers, doctors, radiologists, lawyers, or architects that they can be retrained for better careers when they've already been to college, apprenticed, and interned and now are in desirable and well-paying positions? What are they going to be offered in the way of a better job? When free-traders like Glassman say, "**Don't worry**, we retrained blacksmiths after the advent of automobiles," they're talking about a move from one kind of production to a new one. We didn't just stop using horses and wait around for a better form of transportation, it had already arrived. That, however, is what's happening with Out-sourcing of American jobs. American CEOs are Out-sourcing high paying service and professional jobs, yet there isn't a new job that is attracting labor, at least not in this our country, America.

Blacksmiths didn't lose their livelihood and then wait years for the introduction of the automobile. The automobile industry that forced blacksmiths and carriage makers out of business simultaneously created new jobs. Americans are not losing their jobs to a dynamic, rapidly changing economy. Americans are losing jobs because we permit U.S. multinationals to force American workers to compete with cheap-cost foreign labor.

Un-truth No. 7: Out-sourcing benefits everyone. Look at what happens when Honda Out-sources to the United States and builds cars in the U.S.A. The United States is In-sourcing as many jobs as it's Out-sourcing.

"In-sourcing," as, the multinationals, and other free-traders like to call the building of foreign factories in this country, is a sham, and a bamboozled argument. Honda, Toyota, and BMW, for example, built plants here to win access to the world's richest car markets. That required them to make an investment in American-based facilities and American workers. There is no similarity of any kind between the foreign companies' and CEOs hiring of Americans to staff these "transplants" and the Out-sourcing of American jobs to **India** or other third world countries simply to take advantage of cheap-cost labor, rather than enter a foreign market. The hiring of American workers in plants owned by foreign companies is not analogous in any way to IBM's CEO shipping 10,000 jobs to India solely for the purpose of paying lower wages.

As I've mentioned, under the direction of the Reagan Administration, the U.S. Congress and U.S. trade administration and free-trade proponents like to call "**In-sourcing**" is really just foreign direct investment in the United States. Those foreign-based companies build here, and they sell here. They don't build cars here and then send those cars back to Japan or Germany for sale. They are building here to get access to our market, and they're doing a good job of it. On the other hand, our trade agreements rarely open up foreign markets to the degree that the United States has opened up its markets. We don't sell into those other markets, because we can't.

Un-truth No. 8: The goal of Out-sourcing jobs overseas is to increase productivity, not simply to cut wage costs. Out-sourcing proponents claim that it's all about productivity, not price. Almost everyone agrees that the American worker is the most highly productive worker in the world-and among the costliest. But for reasons of public relations, U.S. multinationals are loath to say they're jobs simply to cut their labor costs. No, instead they or their consultants say they're shipping jobs to cheap-cost foreign labor markets to achieve "efficiency" or "higher productivity" or to raise their competitiveness. Nonsense. It's like the old saying: "When they say that ain't the price man, it's the price."

To achieve lower labor costs, the U.S. multinationals are using their corporate consultants, such as **Accenture, McKinsey, and others**, to dress up the language and their rationale. And the consultants are being paid handsomely to do so. But the simple truth is that American CEOs are in crisis mode, and multinationals and our elected officials who support them without reservation are callously and shamelessly selling out the American worker.

Un-truth No. 9: When Corporate America Out-sources jobs overseas, it enlarges its knowledge base and creates not only more jobs here but high-value jobs.

Mr. John Castellani, President of the Business Roundtable, said in 2004, "Shifting routine computer programming, back-office, and call-center jobs overseas does reduce the number of American jobs in those areas, but the cost savings generates new capital to finance the remarkable ingenuity of our economic system, to create new, higher-wage jobs here in the United States." That's the world we all wish we lived in. Sometimes I wonder if there is a heaven will the gate wide-open for CEOs that are in crisis mode? The problem is, there is absolutely no empirical evidence or data to support the statement. In fact, jobs lost are being replaced by lower paying jobs. Maybe some CEOs need to be fired or given some of those "higher-wage jobs" that they are proposing and see how it feels.

Mr. Tom Donohue, president and CEO of the largest business organization in the country, the U.S. Chamber of Commerce, says that the United States also gains technical knowledge by Out-sourcing jobs. Now…Tom is one of the smartest and most aggressive spokespersons for any cause or group in Washington, and a likeable fellow. But he's just plain foolish to think this way, and simply wrong in his statement. Knowledge and expertise are moving from the United States to the cheap-cost foreign labor markets along with our jobs faster than your cat can catch her tail, and where Out-sourcing our technology advantage. Remember America is at war with terrorism!

Un-truth No. 10: We want to see countries like India prosper. Out-sourcing helps their economies and their workers.

I really hope that none of the people who use this argument are suggesting that we create a middle class anywhere in the world at the expense of our own? Because for those who live and work here in America, for those who run companies based here in America, their first and foremost national concern should be the welfare of their own nation first, America. As far as I'm concerned, there's no way you can help build your neighbor's house when your own is on fire and burning to the ground, with no fire department.

Certainly we must aid other countries, we are a giving and helpful nation but that doesn't mean we need to send our jobs to them at the expense of our own prosperity. There are other ways to provide aid. The elitist surely won't continue to demand that we consign our workers to an ongoing labor competition with China, the Philippines, India, Haiti, and Mexico. Those who claim that we have a higher responsibility to the world economy than to American workers might consider a visit to their local unemployment office to talk with a few of the people in the lines. Our highest responsibility is to preserve the American Dream for all Americans.

Un-truth No. 11: U.S. multinationals are Out-sourcing because Americans aren't well enough educated to fill the jobs.

First, it's simply untrue. The more jobs Corporate American CEOs Out-sources, the fewer workers to pay local, state, and federal taxes, which further punishes our struggling public education system. As Corporate America is fond of saying, companies don't pay taxes; people do. And if people don't have jobs, our tax base diminishes, and we have less to support public education. U.S. multinationals should be spending money, and setting up training for public school students, and volunteering to work in our schools, rather than lamenting the poor quality of education. In fact, we all should be doing far more to improve our public schools. But the Out-sourcing of American jobs is worsening our problems, not solving them. The law of supply and demand will always determine economic choices. As Corporate America recruits more labor from third world countries, it is encouraging our young people to make educational choices that may be ominous for our ability to produce and for our future prosperity, our children, that includes the children of American CEOs. This past year enrollments in computer engineering jobs dropped 26 percent. MIT, arguably one of the most prestigious schools in the world, announced that enrollment in its engineering programs has dropped 37 percent in the past two years. Chinese schools now graduate more than 374,000 engineers every year, far above the approximately 91,000 who graduate annually from American institutions.

I hear some of the world's biggest technology companies bragging about the amount of money they spend on research and development. But they don't always make the distinction between R & D that's going on in this country and R & D that's going on in newly created facilities in other countries-facilities that house the labor that is replacing American workers. As we know, **Microsoft** pledged $400 million last year to create resources in **India,** on top of some $750 million it had already promised to **China.** That's more than a billion dollars that Microsoft has put into other countries while thousands of software programmers in the United States, still home to Microsoft, go looking for work.

Un-truth No. 12: U.S. companies have to compete in a world market. Even if everyone agreed that Out-sourcing is terrible, there's no way to stop it.

This is the fatalism defense of Out-sourcing. The multinationals say there's no practical way to end Out-sourcing. The reality is that we could end it tomorrow. Mr. Bruce Josten, executive vice president of the U.S. Chamber of Commerce, said that "the issue was complicated and that his members were still trying to figure out the ramifications, the laws, and the actual numbers of employees directly affected."

What about a moratorium on Out-sourcing by Corporate American CEOs until his colleagues worked out the details with Congress and academia. Mr. Josten's reply-"he'd rather see Congress pass tort-reform and rather we had a moratorium on politicians at the state level introducing bills to stop Out-sourcing." In other words, no moratorium on Out-sourcing, even though that would at least temporarily halt the practice and give us the time necessary to determine how many jobs have been shipped out of the country and how many more are at risk, and time to create a national policy on the subject. But of course, that's the real point: Corporate **American CEOs** can do better but doesn't want the public to know the real numbers, or the real impact, and the last thing it wants is a national policy on the issue.

All these Un-truths and the facts that dispel them have been part of the early stages of a public dialogue, from the factory-floors and meeting rooms in America, from the floor of the U.S. Senate to the water cooler and even in the warm water restrooms. Despite the extraordinary efforts of the multinationals, their lobbyists, and the politicians they support to distort the debate on the critical issue of Out-sourcing, I believe that nearly all working Americans understand that not only truth is being "tainted" but also our economic future and our way of life, the American dream for all Americans.

7

The Un-truths of Out-sourcing and Free-trade

A man or woman willing to work and unable to find work is perhaps the saddest sight to see and cripples vision and destroys family values.

—WAYNE HOLOVACS

Many Americans who find themselves unemployed are often in need of government assistance. They use state run programs, usually in the form of call-services, where they can apply for and collect benefits over the phone. The states fund these services with taxpayer money, the goal being to make sure that people in the state are cared for and employed. After all, when people are off the welfare or unemployment rolls, it results in more taxes for the entire state. California, where I lived allot of my life, alone spends $400 million running just one of these programs.

Yet the people who are getting paid to help the unemployed in California aren't even California state workers. **WHAT! Did you say?...Rather, they're residents of India and Mexico.** They're cheap-cost foreign laborers, being paid with California tax dollars to answer the telephone when unemployed Californians need help. California is not the only state engaging in this practice of Out-sourcing state programs. Ms. Stella Hopkins of the *Charlotte Observer* conducted a fascinating survey that found that forty states, as well as the District of Columbia, have food stamp help desks that use operators in other countries.

Why are states staffing these employment services with cheap-cost overseas labor when the goal is to help get their own residents back into the workforce? The logic behind this escapes me at every level of my being. In fact, it escapes just about everyone who gives it a moment of thought. The reason is obvious. As Kerry Korpi, of the American Federation of State, County and Municipal Employees said, "This was a program that's set up to help people who can't find a job." **So, Americans calling for help on food stamps and they're calling India.** It's a cruel irony. Being kicked when your down.

If, instead, that job was located here in the United States of America, maybe there would be one less person who needed food stamps. **American State Out-sourcing** is doubly damaging in that the **use** of **foreign labor** distances the states from the people they are supposed to serve. It affects residents on a personal level. When someone calls, say, a food stamp help desk, how is a customer service representative located on the other side of the world going to instruct them about how to go to a particular nearby market that takes food stamps, or which subway or bus line will take them there? Out-sourcing jobs that are designed for the well-being of American state residents raises the depersonalization and humiliation of the Out-sourcing process to a whole new level of American pain and suffering for no good reason.

Using taxpayer dollars to pay foreign workers is creating a lot of angry voters, and rightfully so. Washington State came under fire when it was revealed that not only were the phone service operators of its food stamp program based in Bangalore, India, but the software programming for the Washington State Health Care Authority was being coded in part in Hyderabad. Mr. Tom Fitzsimmons, the governor's chief of staff, defended the practice, stating, "**We want the most value for our technology investment. And the most value adds up to perhaps including teams of vendors that include capacities from Off-shore.**" That must have been cold comfort to Washington's out-of-work software programmers giving American technology away by a state official.

But Washington is learning that Out-sourcing doesn't always live up to its promise of being quick, efficient, and cheap in labor cost. The Indian subcontractor building Washington's new health authority software has repeatedly delayed delivery.

As I noted earlier, Indiana's Department of Workforce Development (DWD) signed a $15+ million contract with one of India's most prominent Out-sourcing firms, Tata, that's right Tata. The contract was slated to bring seventy-five Indian workers, who work at a reduced wage, to Indiana to develop new computer programs that would replace the state's existing tax and unemployment claims processing system. When word of the deal leaked out, citizens and legislators were incensed, in no small part because the (DWI) **is charged with helping Indiana**

workers find jobs. Within a month of the deal, Indiana governor Mr. Joe Kernan had the contract canceled under a new initiative called **"Opportunity Indiana."** Such moves have yet to stem the tide. Proponents of Out-sourcing state jobs claim that Out-sourcing saves the taxpayers money because they can provide the services for a reduced rate. But proponents can't quantify those savings across the board. In fact, if they had given those call-center jobs to people living within the state, those people would be paying taxes back to the state. That strikes me and, I hope, most people, as a win-win solution for the state and its citizens. Because, people in other countries don't pay taxes to the United States. That money goes overseas and stays there.

Who would resist giving those jobs to state workers and providing such an obvious benefit to our states? Well, one is Mr. **Harry Miller, President of the Information Technology Association of America** (**ITAA**), the leading trade association for the IT industry. <u>**Miller wants to make sure that Out-sourcing isn't stifled by any government attempts to keep the jobs at home.**</u> Mr. (President) Miller refers to a "study showing that Off-shore competition added ninety thousand, more jobs to the U.S. last year, will add three hundred thousand jobs to the U.S. by the year 2008. We don't need this kind of restriction legislation." That may be **the result of his group's study, but that's all it is**, a study by a special-interest group. I don't think his logic would sway American workers who are in need of jobs and would be happy to be doing the jobs that are shipped to other countries.

Another group that doesn't like the idea of keeping those jobs here is the **National Foundation for American Policy**. That group, whose board includes former aides to Vice President Cheney, and former President Reagan, released a study that claims that legislation to block the shipment of American jobs to cheap-cost foreign labor markets is unconstitutional. **Knowing this should make you want to call someone.** However, Mr. Stuart Anderson, the director of this organization, confirms that the courts have found that states don't have the right to make their own foreign policy or their own trade agreements or trade policies, that in doing so, states are contravening existing U.S. trade agreements and making their own foreign commerce decisions. He also confirms that states like California could face trade retaliation. Anderson believes that "belligerent activity" like restricting Out-sourcing deals will only do harm to our nation, but it will be you the American public to decide and for American CEOs to consider.

It's hard to see what type of retaliation countries like India, Thailand, the Philippines, or Romania would inflict on California. Would they stop Out-sourcing their jobs over here? Since they don't Out-source to us, that's not an issue. The real issue is that those countries have bid on state, not federal contracts and have won them at the expense of American jobs. Not to mention that awarding those contracts overseas contributes to our out-of-wack trade deficit.

But Mr. Anderson believes that the trade deficit is good for workers because, "When you look at France and Germany, they have a trade surplus. And because of the inflexible labor markets they have twice the unemployment rate as the U.S.... The U.S. actually has a surplus in white-collar services we sell abroad. So, we have actually more to lose in retaliation."

The fact is, that surplus has decreased by 36 percent. Our deficit has increased dramatically. To my mind, it may be time for our American CEOs to get "belligerent, bold, and American" and start leveling the playing field. Mr. Anderson, however, makes the case that the United States benefits from lower prices and that the real issue is job training and education. I don't think helping consumers save a few cents on trinkets and T-shirts is worth the loss of American jobs, I could be wrong. And I haven't heard Anderson or anyone else mention about where we're going to get all those jobs that we plan on training everyone for.

To be fair, it seems that many state legislatures were not aware that portions of their food stamp and employment help desks were located in other countries. In many cases, elected officials have tried to act quickly to address the issue. More than two-thirds of our state legislatures are working on bills to limit Out-sourcing of state contracts. Governors in Minnesota, Michigan, Arizona, and North Carolina have bypassed their state legislators and acted on their own to block the Out-sourcing of state jobs. Florida state senator Mr. Walter "Skip" Campbell proposed legislation to stop the Out-sourcing of jobs after the state gave a $280 million contract to Convergys, which maintains call-centers in India. Florida Senator Campbell, like many others, found it reprehensible that Florida taxpayers should have to surrender their tax dollars to keep the economy of India afloat while American states struggle with joblessness. The senator took a personal interest in the issue after his brother-in-law was laid off when his job was sent to India. Mr. Campbell's bill was eventually defeated, in part because of opposition from Governor Mr. Jeb Bush, the president's brother. Something to ponder…A similar bill in New Jersey met the same fate. A bill to ban Out-sourcing of state contracts easily passed that state's senate, with a unanimous vote of 40-0. Then it died in the assembly state government committee, where it sat for over a year without being given a hearing or a vote. A possible reason for its demise was the **Information Technology Association of America**, which opposed the bill and actively lobbied against it. Even if such measures do become law, there will be loopholes large enough to sail a steamer-ship through with many steamer trunks. While many states are trying to **keep state services in America,** a lot of them haven't stipulated that those jobs actually be performed by Americans. This allows **for a form of In-sourcing** that uses foreign workers, not American citizens, to perform jobs. Many of these workers come to the United States using what are known as **H-1 B and L-1 visas**. They are still foreign nationals, and they often work at a fraction of the pay of their American coworkers. Since they aren't American citizens, they don't pay taxes here. Many of them are taught skills while here and then take their expertise and their money and return home. (This most certainly would have been the case with Indiana and its Tata contract.) Even worse, some of this legislation doesn't take into account that while the work is being done in America, it is being done by foreign companies. They don't have to pay into the U.S. tax base, either. What's striking about this dilemma is that so many people still don't get it and still aren't willing to accept it as reality. Mr. Daniel Henninger of the *Wall Street journal* wrote about Out-sourcing, he said, "What's weird is what a lonely fight it turns out to be." To be fair, it appears that many state legislatures were not aware that portions of their food stamp and employment help desks were located in other countries. In many cases, elected officials have tried to act quickly to address the issue. But like so many analysts, journalists, and politicians who aren't willing to face the facts, Mr. Henninger overlooked the fact that Out-sourcing is a very big deal to many people. The proof is evident across the country: As of this writing, thirty-seven states have legislation pending that prohibits the Out-sourcing of state jobs to overseas workforces. Pennsylvania has even gone as far as to create legislation that would require companies (CEOs) that Out-source more than a hundred jobs to a foreign country to disclose that fact. If those companies are Out-sourcing that many jobs, they would not be eligible to receive state aid or state or local contracts for seven years.

The California state senate overwhelmingly approved a bill that would require state contractors to certify that contract work would be done by people living in the state of California. It also approved a second bill in 2004 that would require employers (CEOs) to state the numbers of workers employed in California, other states, and overseas as part of their payroll reports. Maybe there is hope…

But the only state to successfully get anti-Out-sourcing written into law is Tennessee. In early June, last year Governor Mr. Phil Bredesen signed a bill that made Tennessee the first state to give businesses incentives to keep their jobs in the state and not send them overseas. State procurement officials involved in call-center and data-processing bids are to give preference to contractors who agree to use only U.S. workers. The bill had, as you might expect, received strong support from the state's legislators.

Why is Tennessee the only state to have succeeded thus far? Because lobbying pressure has kept other states from passing such laws. They are not interested in what voters want, only in what their corporate members CEOs want. And since lobbying groups don't represent people like you and me, the interests of the vast number of citizens get moved to the side. Lobbyists are committed to the interests of the corporations that pay them, and that's the sum total of their focus. Lobbying firms and corporations may not care about individual citizens, but that doesn't mean they are unaware of us or completely impervious to our criticisms. They watch the news, they read papers, and they are aware that Americans are not happy about the jobs that are being sent overseas. To defuse the Out-sourcing backlash, or sidestep it altogether, a number of companies have created internal guidelines or written memos on how to address the subject. These documents are designed to be used by human resources personnel and management as a way to sanitize the issue for employee consumption. Essentially, such documents are meant to tout the benefits of Out-sourcing for the whole company, while reassuring those remaining employees (who have not been cut, Out-sourced) that their jobs are secure and that the company is committed to them for the long term. Which, as you and I know, lasts only until the next time the American company (CEO) decides cheap-cost labor will improve its balance sheet. These documents and memos are deceptive, and they do nothing to create an honest dialogue with anyone involved in the process. Employees are not informed of the truth, management cowers behind PR-produced spin, and everyone fears the motives of everyone else.

Most recently Hewlett Packard employee's comments and hallway conversations have revealed these facts. The employees worry that management will ax them at the drop of a hat, while management fears that employees may quit over their treatment or, worse, sabotage operations if they feel they are being exploited. The lack of openness in dealing with the issue creates a culture of **fear that runs from top to bottom of the company. Company mergers will bring this on as well.**

The fact that **legislators are getting pressure from their voters** is a more important indication. People who are fed up band together and become their own pressure groups, and politicians and American CEOs have to sit up and take notice. While not possessing the same levels of funding that lobbyists can bring to bear, citizens groups can attract enough media attention to make local politicians squirm in their seats.

That's exactly what happened over the past year as state Out-sourcing became headline news. Politicians were taken to task for putting the economic and labor needs of their constituencies dead last. Some of the elected officials initially responded in ways that sounded as though they had their own cheat-sheets. By and large, they eventually had to drop their defenses and address the fiscal downside of the issue. A few politicians, to their credit, stood up right from the start and said that Out-sourcing state jobs was just plain wrong. The groundswell of concern on the part of legislators is a relatively recent phenomenon. The concern is certainly heightened by the fact that we're in and out of an election year, 2004, and a lot of people still don't have jobs in 2005 because of Out-sourcing. Nonetheless, the issue is on the table, and Tennessee's recent ruling on Out-sourcing proves that pro-Out-sourcing lobbyists can't claim total victory-yet.

For the states, there's a long way to go before they resolve the inherent problems that Out-sourcing creates. As states and **American CEOs** deal with the aftermath and (can do better), the a recession look for ways **to correct** their own **budget deficits,** they're putting bigger burdens on their taxpayers. By relying on individual taxpayers and not corporate taxes to make up the shortfall, our government is already squeezing its citizens. Nearly two-thirds of corporations don't pay federal taxes, and many of them enjoy big breaks at the local level, which is meant to help create good, and professional level new jobs.

Out-sourcing may seem like a cheap-cost labor solution to fiscal shortfalls in the near term, but the long-term ramifications are sure to be destructive. Paying millions-or hundreds of millions-of dollars to In-sourced foreign nationals or to overseas laborers ensures that what little money the states do have is on a one-way trip out of our country, America. How can the states hope to recoup lost tax revenue when they aren't making a concerted effort to employ the workers who are on their own unemployment lines?

The solution is a simple equation. If you put a resident of the state to work, that person pays taxes. They are taken off the unemployment rolls and thus do not need state assistance. Employment also increases their purchasing power, adding to the state coffers through sales taxes. The money moves within the state, benefiting everybody in the state.

The inability of state legislatures to prevent this kind of abuse of state workers and taxpayers is one of the most glaring examples yet of the control that companies American CEOs and special interests have over our political agenda. You'd be hard-pressed to find an American worker who agrees with the practice, yet their needs, and their votes have become subservient to the demands of Corporate America. Look no further than the failed New Jersey proposal, which passed without a single dissenting vote yet was setup to fail through the efforts of a group that supports Out-sourcing because it improves the bottom line of its member companies.

America, we're a country, first and foremost, of men, women, and children who should expect that our government and its American CEOs are behaving in our interests at every level, whether it be national, state, county, or town. When people aren't working and are actively being harmed by our government's or corporate policies, then it's obvious that citizens are not the top priority of our elected officials. Corporations are making the decisions for our lawmakers, and maybe we've become incidental.

Until this state of affairs is straightened out, we'll continue to lose jobs to other countries, and our tax base will erode. And when our government wonders why its citizens can no longer carry the tax burden after their jobs are gone, all it will have to do is look at whose interests it has really been serving all these years. Just take a look at the television commercial that display many workers supported one retired person in the 1950's, well that's because the key word is **workers**, **American workers**. There were jobs, good jobs to be found then, and then the commercial goes on to say that Social Security will be supported by Only two or one worker for each retiree in so many years. Well if there are less jobs, that means less money for the social security fund, it's the new math…something to think about.

8

For the Americans?

Its' 2005, The United States of America has become the largest debtor nation on the face of the earth, the largest debtor nation in the history of the world. Our national debt combined with our trade-debt has reached almost the same level as our yearly gross domestic product. Our combined federal budget deficits and trade deficits are approaching 11 percent of GDP. We are writing mountains of IOUs to foreign countries to pay for our excessive spending, both as a government and as consumers. Those IOUs to foreigners are claims on our assets, and they will come due. And although many economists say our debt is not a problem in the long run, I believe the due date will arrive sooner than most of us imagine. China is one of America's largest lender countries. In today's (March 2005) news there is talk of WAR with Taiwan. If that was to happen quick change will be upon us all.

How can the world's wealthiest nation, the world's only superpower, find itself in the grip of such monstrous debt? **First**, our national debt has risen because our government has had to accelerate federal spending to fight the WAR on terrorism and to add expensive social programs. **Second**, because tax revenues have been reduced by tax cuts, which did help, until recently, by slowing economic growth. **Third**, our trade-debt has risen because American consumers are out-of-control. Our household debt is at record levels, personal bankruptcies are at an all-time high, and we continue to buy, and buy voraciously, **CHARGE-IT**, pay later, but remember there are new bankruptcy laws on the books. It will not be easy to claim any longer. And we are **buying imported goods on credit**.

Fourth, and to the point of American CEOs can do better we have the technology, because we have no choice but to buy imported goods, since we don't produce enough products in this country. We're dependent on foreigners not only for our oil and gasoline but for our steel, cement, clothing, lumber, electronic appliances, computers, and a host of other products that we once made in America. And **fifth,** because we don't produce enough goods and services that the rest of the world wants to buy or can buy from us, America.

WHY? Because we don't Out-source as much as we import, we must either slow our international shopping or continue to buy on credit and add further to our trade-debt. In past years we didn't have this problem. Until 1975 we produced and Out-sourced more than we imported.

But in the decades since, we've increased our consumption and reduced our production, at such a staggering rate that we find ourselves under a crushing level of debt. The situation is steadily getting worse, because now we're producing less for ourselves **as well as for our trading partners.**

The **first reason for our failure to compete effectively** is our one-sided and badly negotiated "free" and un-balanced trade agreements. Other countries retain barriers to the goods and services we Out-source, effectively preventing us from paying down that debt with goods that we produce here. Meanwhile, our consumers keep buying imports, and our deficit increases.

The second reason is directly related to Out-sourcing and off-shoring. We're shutting down our domestic factories and sending our jobs overseas. So even if, by some unlikely stroke of national will, or luck, we made a decision to immediately stop buying from foreign countries, we couldn't. We simply don't produce enough of our own goods to meet our own demand. We've reduced manufacturing in industries such as automotive, electronics, timber, and steel to the point that our entire production capacity is too fragile to meet even our own requirements. We've handed those industries, those technologies over to other countries, with full awareness that we will be dependent on them for those goods for the foreseeable future.

Our lack of self-reliance and inability to produce our own goods is seen by most economists as simply a global economy at work, but our growing dependency on the rest of the world for commodities and finished goods alike should be reason enough for considerable concern, if not alarm. Not only is the industrialization of China, much of Asia, and Eastern Europe creating rising demand for commodities and capital, it is now setting the stage for serious global competition that the United States is not in a position to win. Regional trade is rising dramatically, further adding to the contest for raw products and, ultimately, finished products as well. Regional trade in Asia, and countries like India, Korea, and China, rose 48 percent last year. Asian countries and companies are intensifying their search for new and emerging markets for their goods, and they're increasingly turning to their neighbors. The United States may be importing all the goods it wants from these countries right now, but there may come a time when that won't be possible. There is absolutely no assurance that China will always maintain its currency at artificially low levels that allow us to buy their products relatively cheap. And what happens when we have flooded the world with so many American dollars that our currency declines further, making imports even more expensive? And what would happen to our economy if countries that own immense amounts of our securities and debt decide to reduce their holdings? Our economic dependency could carry an extremely high price.

As if it wasn't bad enough that we no longer manufacture goods that are basic to our national needs, Corporate America (CEOs), with the full support of the past two administrations, has begun shipping high-paying jobs to other countries, from legal, research, engineering, new technologies and medical services to accounting, finance, operations, and software development. These are high-end professional and service jobs that the free-traders told us would replace the millions of manufacturing jobs that we've lost.

Not so long ago, those same free-traders were declaring that our Out-sources of high-technology products would one day offset our weak performance in the Out-source of other products. But now the high-technology trade surplus we had as recently as three years ago has turned into a $29.5 billion deficit. Even though we've been running trade deficits in goods and products, we've managed to run a trade surplus in services for years. But now we're losing that advantage as well. America's surplus in the service sector dropped to $60+ billion last year, a significant and worrisome decline from 1998, when we had a $93 billion surplus. Not even the heaviest doses of faith-based free-trade can alter the facts or the predicament in which we now find ourselves.

America's annual trade deficit amounts to 5 percent of our GDP. Estimates by the Economic Policy Institute suggest that 99+ percent of this deficit results from spending on goods and products that we no longer manufacture in the United States. That should be alarming to even the most limited free-trade advocates. Our few attempts to redress the one-sided free-trade agreements with the rest of the world have largely met with failure. The World Trade Organization's 2003 meeting in Cancun was a setup for failure on every count, and the U.S. agenda was effectively derailed. Not that we should expect much from that organization on our behalf: The United States has lost more than 83 percent of the cases in which it has been the defendant before the WTO tribunals, and the WTO has ruled against the United States in more than 91 percent of the cases tried against Asian countries.

Those of us who believe that our government has failed abysmally to enforce environmental and labor standards, to create equitable and balanced trade agreements, and to call for a rational approach to America's trade policies have been called protectionists. Yet no one has leveled this charge at countries that retain significant trade barriers. No one that I know of has called the European Union or Japan protectionist, yet they regularly maintain trade surpluses with the United States. Nor has anyone complained loudly that China doesn't buy enough American products, maintains tariffs that are barriers to U.S. Out-sources, doesn't pay its workers a minimum wage, and fails to enforce workplace safety standards. Instead, American CEOs surrendered to the Chinese on a wide range of commercial issues including contract law, intellectual property rights, and reciprocity. And you won't hear about China's labor regulations and pay, either. That wouldn't be good for business.

Labor organizations in this country have at least tried to stem the exodus of manufacturing jobs and the Out-sourcing of service jobs to cheap-cost labor markets by demanding that our trading partners live up to agreed-upon trade practices that were made conditions of gaining access to our consumer market. The AFL-CIO filed a complaint with the U.S. trade office claiming that China, as a U.S. trade partner, has not lived up to the labor standards of our trade agreements. This includes enforcing the maximum number of hours a laborer (person) is allowed to work, adhering to and enforcing safety standards, and ensuring a minimum wage. Right now China's wages are between 49 and 91 percent lower than they should be, which reduces Chinas production costs and keeps its Out-sources cheaper than they should be. Chinas indifference to labor standards means there is no way that American labor will ever be able to compete with Chinese labor.

The AFL-CIO claimed that the Chinese had cheated on our agreements, and invoked the Trade Act of 1974 and asked the U.S. trade representative to put things right. Specifically, they asked for three things: (1) that the United States impose trade remedies against China that are equal to the amount of revenue gained from the cheating, (2) that the United States fashion an agreement that says our country will reduce these remedies only upon verification of China's meeting the labor benchmarks that have been ignored, and (3) that the United States not enter into any more agreements with the World Trade Organization until the WTO mandates that all its members meet United Nations International Labor Organization standards. The current administration does not support the AFL-CIO position at this time. That wouldn't be good for business or would it? You decide.

And the abundance of ridiculously cheap-cost labor in China is its principal attraction for foreign companies that are investing hundreds of billions of dollars to build plants, factories, and infrastructure in China-and Out-sourcing jobs there by the boatload, like **HP™**, **DELL™**, **INTEL™**, and **MICROSOFT™**. Millions of manufacturing jobs have been effectively shipped to China and other countries, and entire industries in America have been shut down. While the rise in wages of all American workers has been depressed by Off-shoring and Out-sourcing, labor union membership has been the hardest hit. In fact, the unions have been increasingly marginalized in the past three decades. Their influence has diminished as their membership has suffered a dramatic decline, falling by more than half since the late '70s. Despite this drop, Corporate American CEOs are still quick to blame organized labor for its need to Out-source jobs to cheap-cost foreign labor markets. The Out-sourcing American multinational corporations and their consultants say that unions have driven up wages to a point where the only recourse is to move American factories and plants overseas and replace American workers with cheap labor-cost, foreign labor. The multinationals and their consultants also blame our burdensome legal system, high tax rates, excessive workplace regulation, and environmental laws.

There's no question that labor unions became too powerful in the 1960s and '70s in this country, just as I think there's no question that Corporate America CEOs are too powerful now. But everyone acknowledges that almost every benefit that working men and women in this country enjoy is directly attributable to the efforts of labor organizations and unions. Unless a countervailing power to that of Corporate America CEOs asserts themselves, "and do better" the American worker faces less opportunity and lower pay in the years ahead. Labor unions were once that countervailing power, but no longer. They got out negotiated. They should have done a better job at negotiating. They should have done a better job in enforcing the laws. Together, working with CEOs (management), I know this. I know the American worker can compete with anybody in the world. And that's what we want to do just compete, beat them at their own game.

Some folks believe that filing a complaint and demanding sanctions is the only way to stem the tide of job losses this country has experienced in recent years.

The sub-thought here is that American workers can compete if they're willing to accept the low wages-and dismal living conditions-of cheap-cost foreign laborers. And that is certainly the choice that has been forced upon us by Corporate America's CEOs Off-shoring and Out-sourcing of jobs: Either accept lower living standards or begin to balance our trade and restrict Out-sourcing.

Our multinationals want the best of all possible worlds: to draw upon the world's greatest capital markets and enjoy the benefits of the strongest legal, political, and economic systems ever created, while Out-sourcing jobs to cheap-cost labor to overseas markets and selling those goods and services into the richest consumer market in the world. And all that the multinationals are asking of us is that we give up our quality of life, our way of life, for their profitability.

I know of no one, least of all myself, who is recommending that America not trade with the rest of the world. Fair and balanced trade is good for everyone. No one wants America to withdraw from the world of international commerce. The choice we face is whether we will demand reciprocal benefits, mutuality, and balance in our trading relationships or will simply continue policies and practices that strip us of our wealth and destroy our American way of life. That choice, is clear.

What is not clear is whether Americans will demand that our corporate CEOs, our government *make* the correct choice. We find ourselves confronted with a number of difficult choices today and in the months and years ahead, choices that will likely determine our economic future, the kind of society we, our children will live in, and our nation's role in the world. And the choices are made more difficult by our reluctance to engage in a public dialogue dealing with the real issues and to discuss possible answers to questions that, apparently, Corporate America and Washington would prefer not even be asked.

I believe these are some of the most critical issues, to pose the tough questions raised by the Out-sourcing of American jobs to cheap-cost foreign labor markets and by the slow but steady pace forward wholesale pursuit of free-trade agreements. While Out-sourcing has cost hundreds of thousands of jobs, millions more are at risk. Today I watched on the television, Mickey "Ds", McDonalds will be "Out-sourcing" its drive through service order window to North Dakota U.S.A, maybe there is light at the end of this tunnel or maybe not, you decide…

9

An American CEOs Choice

While we pursue free-trade, our status as the world's largest debtor nation worsens. Even if the result is more profits for multinational corporations, do we truly believe that Out-sourcing those jobs will lead to a better life in this country, America, for our workers? Even if we are buying more and cheap-cost labor goods from our trading partners, do we really believe that our quality of life is better and that we should sustain permanent dependency and indebtedness? Or will Out-sourcing and free-trade lead to further, wider gaps between the wealthy and our middle class? Should we simply hope that Corporate America, our American CEOs and government laws will find a social conscience and voluntarily restrain its Out-sourcing to a minimum? Or at least be fair and balanced. Should we continue to permit the Out-sourcing of our knowledge base, Americas intellectual properties, technology, and capital to other countries to provide the products and services for sale back to America? **"Remember the world is at war with terrorism"**. **China and Taiwan are ready to fight...** Or should we rely on public policy, regulation, tariffs, and quotas to protect our standard of living? Or should we share the blind faith of many in Corporate America and Washington, in the power of a free-market to resolve these questions?

Federal Reserve chairman Alan Greenspan is a keeper of that faith. In late 2004, talking again about the relationship between anemic job creation and the Out-sourcing of American jobs, Greenspan said, "In response to these strains and the dislocations they cause, a new round of protectionist steps is being proposed. These alleged cures would make matters worse rather than better. They would do little to create jobs; and if foreigners were to retaliate, we would surely lose jobs. Besides enhancing education, we need to further open markets here and abroad to allow our workers to compete effectively in the global marketplace." Education is certainly a critical component of any long-term strategy to improve our competitiveness, but it's an impossibility as a short-term strategy, and the threat of Out-sourcing American workers is immediate, right now. But for what jobs and careers would the Fed chairman have us "enhance education"? It is not as if Out-sourcing is only affecting uneducated Americans-quite the contrary.

The unemployment statistics for workers in the computer science industries, for instance, are nothing short of shocking. The unemployment rate for computer hardware engineers in the United States is a staggering 13 percent.

We shouldn't be overly surprised that our leaders and institutions have produced very few answers to the most important questions we face today. Our collective reflex has been either to ignore the challenges of the world as it is or to assume, whether out of ideology, political faith, or sheer apathy, that the world we want will one day arrive. And while we don't have as much information and evidence as we would like, that will always be the case.

Lack of information isn't a sufficient reason to ignore the evidence we do have about the impact of our free-trade policies and Out-sourcing, or In-sourcing to avoid considering whether we could better serve our CEOs, national economic, social, and political interests; nor is it sufficient reason to further defer our judgment on the kind of society and nation that will result from continuing current policies versus setting a new, better path. I have no doubt whatsoever that the United States must pursue a new direction in our trade policies, seek fair and balanced international trade, and end the wholesale Out-sourcing of American jobs. Our political leaders will set that direction, and the choices that voters make are more important than ever in determining whether we will succeed in setting a new course before it's too late. But it is the American CEO that can help immediately before government steps in, **American CEOs** can do better, we have the technology. Take the first step today and reverse this terrible pain to America, your country. Lead your American company into victory, that is part of your American spirit and do not surrender your homeland for because of cheap foreign labor. Every American CEO knows that it is what's inside of you that makes a business successful. Set the new standard and ADVERTISE IT, the CEO who does this will become a hero, move the company forward and make profit. Stand-up

and be proud that you're an American company and your partners are internationally known and you all work together for the
common good of fair and balanced trade. American CEOs
should help each-other. Turn away from countries that practice
"slave-labor" before more American companies are tagged with
that label. Remember American CEOs live in American, its
your homeland too. While writing this book I came across
information that was very disappointing, March 18th, 2005 and
a body-blow to America, Americans will probably not hear
about unless your on the inside. IBM…an Icon of American
technology and services, that should be a leader and not a fol-
lower is replacing its decision-making-senior-management levels
with In-sourced-foreign-cheap-labor into America. IBM cannot
find an American citizen that is qualified enough to be given
this opportunity. In my opinion, this is shameful. Should
American continue to be a customer of IBM? You decide…

As the boomerang era steps in, It is now clear that most
Republicans and Democrates will support free-trade at any cost
and not temper their commitment to the WTO, NAFTA,
CAFTA, or FTAA, will continue to drive free-trade agreements
that will only worsen our trade deficit, and that most
Democrates will in no way lessen their endorsement of the Out-
sourcing practices of U.S. multinationals. It is also clear that
Corporate America will not end the Out-sourcing of American
jobs to cheap-cost foreign labor markets without government
intervention. But, Our only hope today and into the near future
is our **American CEOs** that to do better we have the technol-

ogy, to be a responsible corporate citizen of The United States of America, soon.

However, It is not clear what the Democrats will do. The New Democrat Clinton administration brought us NAFTA and the WTO. The Democratic party for the past decade and a half has all but abandoned its commitment to working men and women and embraced the New Democrat philosophy. Senator Kerry has supported free-trade, but also has tried to move closer to his party's traditional position on labor. The senator's lambasting of "Benedict Arnold CEOs" who Out-source American jobs put him at the forefront of those supporting workers during the 2004 election.

The conventional wisdom of Corporate America our CEOs and Washington held that there was no reason to worry about millions of American manufacturing jobs lost to cheap-cost overseas markets, because the United States was in transition from a manufacturing economy to a service economy. Growth in our service sector would be so strong that these manufacturing jobs would be replaced by high-value service jobs. But not only has that not happened, our trade surplus in services is actually falling, down by 38 percent since 1996. They were WRONG! **Our American CEOs** can do better we have the technology.

The first requirement of any short-term solution is to see the world as it is, not as Corporate America and Washington tell us it is. American jobs continue to be Out-sourced; our trade deficit continues to worsen. Congress must act now. Corporate America will not end Out-sourcing on its own, unless our

American CEOs start the process: It is driven to cut costs and boost short-term profits, and it will continue to claim that even if it ends the practice of Out-sourcing, its competitors will continue to Out-source and In-source. They're probably right about that. So let's level the **playing field.** Congress and all state governments should immediately prohibit the Out-sourcing of government contracts and American jobs to cheap-cost foreign labor. Some state legislators have introduced bills requiring that work on state government contracts be performed by Americans, but what is needed most is action at the federal level. Remember we are at War with terrorism. While it may be more difficult to regulate the Off-shore Out-sourcing or In-sourcing activities of multinational corporations, our own government should not be spending Americans' tax dollars to send government work abroad. Our costly "free-trade" agreements should be reviewed by Congress and action taken. Our negotiators allowed them to have a 25 percent tariff on U.S. cars being shipped into China, and only a 2.5 percent tariff on any Chinese cars that would be shipped into America." Our trade deficit with Japan totaled $68 billion last year; our deficit with China, $129 billion. In our pursuit of free-trade at all costs, we have given away much more than we have gained. U.S. companies can easily send both their manufacturing and service jobs Off-shore and then re-import their own products and services with nearly un-restricted access to the U.S. marketplace. That exploitation of our trade policies must end. There is simply no way the American worker can compete with third world cheap-labor and some times referred to as "**slave-labor**".

We must also reexamine our relationship with the World
Trade Organization. We should be seeking to raise the standard
of living globally, not reducing American standards to those of a
third world country.

And we should insist that any U.S. multinational that Out-
sources jobs should meet the same privacy standards for its
American customers as if its operations were based here. Unfortunately, current federal privacy laws do not protect individuals
when foreign companies misuse their personal information.
This is something that absolutely must change. Several lawmakers, including U.S. senators Dianne Feinstein (Democrat,
California) and Hillary Clinton (Democrat, New York), in
2005 are pushing legislation to protect American consumers
against such abuses. Congress must pass federal legislation to
better safeguard information sent overseas. Doing so will be
another important step in dissuading U.S. multinationals from
sending American information and jobs abroad.

Several opponents of Out-sourcing, including Senator John
Kerry, have proposed "right-to-know" legislation for call-center
employees. Such rules would require that workers in other parts
of the world identify where they are when speaking with American customers. It would also allow consumers to make their
own determination about whether they want to share private
information with workers on the other side of the globe. It's
unlikely this legislation will have a significant effect, but it could
slow Out-sourcing and In-sourcing at least marginally. A recent
survey conducted by Diamond Cluster International found that
more than 70 percent of IT executives are afraid of the negative

publicity associated with Out-sourcing. We must provide more of an incentive to keep jobs here at home, America. Senator Mr. John Kerry has also proposed, in addition to several other measures, tax incentives for companies keeping American jobs at home. As part of the plan, companies creating more jobs than their previous twelve month average would receive a refund of the payroll taxes of the new employees for two years. But, unfortunately he has not gotten a bill passed for more than 20 years in the Senate. Something to think about…

Several state governors are pressing both the Bush administration and lawmakers on Capitol Hill to take similar action. The government should be working to **monitor** the use of **H-1 B and L-1 visas** by companies that have been charged with using them to hire foreign labor at lower wages than their American counterparts. Not only should the use of these visas be carefully monitored, but considerable research should be done to assess both their impact on our labor market, and the value to the businesses who hire these visa holders. **American Drivers-licenses** are in the spot-light as well. It is the one document that allowed the 9/11 to happen. That one document gave access to most anything in America. You decide? Today, Remember the world is at war with terrorism, and our **American CEOs** must be responsible and act as good corporate American citizens. Reversing decades of unfair free trade at any cost policies, destructive un-fair free-trade agreements, and chronic trade deficits will require first an honest public debate and then tough political and public choices. But our American mistakes are reversible. We still have our destiny in our hands. Our

American CEOs can do better we have the technology. Free-traders believe that we can't alter the policies that led to this dangerous juncture, that only a free market can resolve the problems facing us. Their views that this country should simply accept market forces and America be held-hostage, that we don't require a fair and balanced trade strategy are to me nothing less than setting America up for complete failure, we must take responsibility for our economic future. Determinism and determination have driven our nation's achievements and success for two centuries. Let's hope the same will be said of this century. Just as **American CEOs** can do better we have the technology is published take a look at this report: **Its time for change...YOU DECIDE.**

-**From Red Herring**, an interesting piece on Out-sourcing. Fast Stats: Out-sourcing, bad math...Savings don't add up to much with Out-sourcing: **March 8, 2005** MISCALCU-LATED? Out-sourcing might not be the cost-saving, headache-lifting miracle it's been made out to be. "**Gartner announced this week that Out-sourced customer service operations cost 30 percent more than the top quartile of in-house customer service operations.**" The worldwide market for customer service Out-sourcing should grow about 45 percent from 2004 to 2007, reaching $12.2 billion, but customer defections and hidden costs like in-house backup support often outweigh the potential savings of 25 to 30 percent, says the research firm. Though Off-shore Out-sourcing gets a lot of attention, it will hold its small market share, reaching just 5 percent in 2007. **Seventy percent of the top 15 Indian business-process Out-**

sourcing startups should be acquired, merge, or disappear in 2005.

SOURCE: **Gartner**

Bring it on **American CEOs** can do better we have the technology, MAYBE HOPE IS ALIVE!

APPENDIX

The List

List below are companies we have confirmed as **American CEOs** can do better we have the technology as of this writing, these are U.S. companies either sending American jobs overseas or choosing to employ cheap-cost overseas labor In-sourcing, instead of offering those jobs to American workers. March, _2005_

3Com

3M

Aalfs Manufacturing

Aavid Thermal Technologies

ABC-NACO

Accenture

Access Electronics

Accuride Corporation

Accuride International

Adaptec

ADC

Adobe Air

Adobe Systems

Advanced Energy Industries

Aei Acquisitions

Aetna

Affiliated Computer Services

AFS Technologies

A.G. Edwards

Agere Systems

Agilent Technologies

AIG

Alamo Rent A Car

Albany International Corp.

Albertson's

Alcoa

Alcoa Fujikura

Allen Systems Group

Alliance Fiber Optic Products, Inc.

Alliance Semiconductor

Allstate

Alpha Thought Global

Altria Group

Amazon.com

AMD

Americ Disc

American Dawn

American Express

American Greetings

American Household

American Management Systems

American Standard

American Tool

American Uniform Company

AMETEK

AMI DODUCO

Amloid Corporation

Amphenol Corp.

Analog Devices

Anchor Glass Container

ANDA Networks

Anderson Electrical Products

Andrew Corporation

Angelica Corporation

Anheuser-Busch

Ansell Health Care

Ansell Protective Products

Anvil Knitwear

AOL

A.O. Smith

Apparel Ventures, Inc.

Apple

Applied Materials

Arkansas General Industries

Ark-Les Corporation

Arlee Home Fashions

Artex International

Art Leather Manufacturing

ArvinMeritor

Asco Power Technologies

Ashland

Astenjohnson

Asyst Technologies

AT&T

AT&T Wireless

Atchison Products, Inc.

A.T Cross

A.T Kearney

Augusta Sportswear

Authentic Fitness Corporation

Automatic Data Processing

Avanade

Avanex

Avaya

Avery Dennison

Axiohm Transaction Solutions

Azima Healthcare Services

Ball Corporation

Bank of America

Bank of New York

Bank One

Bard Access Systems

Barnes Group

Barth & Dreyfuss of California

Bassett Furniture

Bassler Electric Company

BBi Enterprises L.P.

Beacon Blankets

BearingPoint

Bear Stearns

BEA Systems

Bechtel

Becton Dickinson

BellSouth

Bentley Systems

Berdon LLP

Berne Apparel

Bernhardt Furniture

Besler Electric Company

Best Buy

Bestt Liebco Corporation

Beverly Enterprises

Birdair, Inc.

BISSELL

Black & Decker

Blauer Manufacturing

Blue Cast Denim

BMC Software

Bobs Candies

Boeing

Borden Chemical

Bose Corporation

Bourns

Bowater

Braden Manufacturing

Brady Corporation

Briggs Industries

Bristol-Myers Squibb

Bristol Tank & Welding Co.

Brocade

Brooks Automation

Brown Wooten Mills Inc.

Buck Forkardt, Inc.

Bumble Bee

Burle Industries

Burlington House Home Fashions

Burlington Northern and Santa Fe Railway

C&D Technologies

Cadence Design Systems

Cains Pickles

Camfil Farr

Candle Corporation

Capital Mercury Apparel

Capital One

Cardinal Brands

Carrier

Carter's

Caterpillar

C-COR.net

Cellpoint Systems

Cendant

Centis, Inc.

Cerner Corporation

Charles Schwab

The Cherry Corporation

ChevronTexaco

CIBER

Ciena

Cigna

Circuit City, Inc.

Cirrus Logic

Cisco Systems

Citigroup

Clear Pine Mouldings

Clorox

CNA

Coastcast Corp.

Coca-Cola

Cognizant Technology Solutions

Collins & Aikman

Collis, Inc.

Columbia House

Columbia Showcase & Cabinet Company

Columbus MCICnnon

Comcast Holdings

Comdial Corporation

CompuServe

Computer Associates

Computer Horizons

Computer Sciences Corporation

Concise Fabricators

Conectl Corporation

Conseco

Consolidated Metro

Consolidated Ventura

Continental Airlines

Cooper Crouse-Hinds

Cooper Industries

Cooper Tire & Rubber

Cooper Tools

Cooper Wiring Devices

Copperweld

Cordis Corporation

Corning

Corning Cable Systems

Corning Frequency Control

Countrywide Financial

COVAD Communications

Covansys

Creo Americas

Cross Creek Apparel

Crouzet Corporation

Crown Holdings

CSX

Cummins

Cutler-Hammer

Cypress Semiconductor

Dana Corporation

Daniel Woodhead

Davis Wire Corp.

Daws Manufacturing

Dayton Superior

DeCrane Aircraft

Delco Remy

Dell Computer

DeLong Sportswear

Delphi

Delta Air Lines

Delta Apparel

DIRECTV

Discover

DJ Orthopedics

Document Sciences Corporation

Dometic Corp.

Donaldson Company

Douglas Furniture of California

Dow Chemical

Dresser

Dun & Bradstreet

DuPont

Earthlink

Eastman Kodak

Eaton Corporation

Edco, Inc.

Editorial America

Edscha

eFunds

Ehlert Tool Company

Elbeco Inc.

Electroglass

Electronic Data Systems

Electronics for Imaging

Electro Technology

Eli Lilly

Elmer's Products

E-Loan

EMC

Emerson Electric

Emerson Power Transmission

Emglo Products

Engel Machinery

En Pointe Technologies

Equifax

Ernst & Young

Essilor of America

Ethan Allen

Evenflo

Evergreen Wholesale Florist

Evolving Systems

Evy of California

Expedia

Extrasport

ExxonMobil

Fairfield Manufacturing

Fair Isaac

Fansteel Inc.

Farley's & Sathers Candy Co.

Fasco Industries

Fawn Industries

Fayette Cotton Mill

FCI USA

Fedders Corporation

Federal Mogul

Federated Department Stores

Fellowes

Fender Musical Instruments

Fidelity Investments

Financial Technologies International

Findlay Industries

First American Title Insurance

First Data

First Index

Fisher Hamilton

Flowserve

Fluidmaster

Fluor

FMC Corporation

Fontaine International

Ford Motor

Foster Wheeler

Franklin Mint

Franklin Templeton

Freeborders

Frito-Lay

Fruit of the Loom

Garan Manufacturing

Gateway

GE

Capital

GE Medical Systems

Gemtron Corporation

General Binding Corporation

General Cable Corp.

General Electric General Motors

Generation 2 Worldwide

Genesco

Georgia-Pacific

Gerber

Childrenswear

Gillette

Global Power Equipment Group.

Globespan

Goldman Sachs Gold Toe Brands

Goodrich Goodyear Tire & Rubber

Google

Graphic Controls

Greenpoint Mortgage

Greenwood Mills

Grote Industries

Grove U.S. LLC

Guardian Life Insurance

Guilford Mills

Gulfstream Aerospace Corp.

Haggar

Halliburton

Hamilton Beach/Procter Silex

Harper-Wyman Company

The Hartford Financial Services Group

Hasbro Manufacturing Services

Hawk Corporation

Hawker Power Systems, Inc.

Haworth

Headstrong

Healthaxis

Hedstrom

Hein-Werner Corp.

Helen of Troy

Helsapenn Inc.

Hershey

Hewitt Associates

Hewlett-Packard

Hoffman Enclosures, Inc.

Hoffman/New Yorker

The Holmes Group

Home Depot

The HON Company

Honeywell

HSN

Hubbell Inc.

Humana

Hunter Sadler

Hutchinson Sealing Systems, Inc.

HyperTech Solutions

IBM

iGate Corporation

Illinois Tool Works

IMI Cornelius

Imperial Home Decor Group

Indiana Knitwear Corp.

IndyMac Bancorp

Infogain

Ingersoll-Rand

Innodata Isogen

Innova Solutions

Insilco Technologies

Intel

InterMetro Industries

International Paper

Interroll Corporation

Intesys Technologies

Intuit

Invacare

Iris Graphics, Inc.

Isola Laminate Systems

Iteris Holdings, Inc.

ITT Educational Services

ITT Industries

Jabil Circuit

Jacobs Engineering

Jacuzzi

Jakel Inc.

JanSport

Jantzen Inc.

JDS Uniphase

Jockey International

John Crane

John Deere

Johns Manville

Johnson & Johnson

Johnson Controls

JPMorgan Chase

J.R. Simplot

Juniper Networks

Justin Brands

K2 Inc.

KANA Software

Kaiser Permanente

Kanbay

Kayby Mills of North Carolina

Keane

Kellogg

Kellwood

KEMET

KEMET Electronics

Kendall Healthcare

Kenexa

Kentucky Apparel

Kerr-McGee Chemical

KeyCorp

Key Industries

Key Safety Systems

KeyTronic Corp.

Kimberly-Clark

KLA-Tencor

Knight Textile Corp.

Kojo Worldwide Corporation

Kraft Foods

Kulicke and Soffa

Kwikset

LaCrosse Footwear

L.A. Darling Company

Lake Village Industries

Lamb Technicon

Lancer Partnership

Lander Company

Lands' End

Lau Industries

Lawson Software

Layne Christensen

Leach International

Lear Corporation

Leech Tool & Die Works

Lehman Brothers

Leoni Wiring Systems

Levi Strauss

Leviton Manufacturing Co.

Lexmark International

Lexstar Technologies

Liebert Corporation

Lifescan

Lillian Vernon

Linksys

Linq Industrial Fabrics, Inc.

Lionbridge Technologies

Lionel

Littelfuse

LiveBridge

LNP Engineering Plastics

Lockheed Martin

Longaberger

Louisiana-Pacific Corporation

Louisville Ladder Group LLC

Lowe's

Lucent

Lund International

Lyall Alabama

Madill Corporation

Magma Design Automation

Magnequench

Magnetek

Maidenform

Mallinckrodt, Inc.

The Manitowoc Company

Manugistics

Marathon Oil

Marine *Accessories Corp.*

Maritz

Marko Products, Inc.

Mars, Inc.

Marshall Fields

Master Lock

Materials Processing, Inc.

Mattel

Maxim Integrated Products

Maxi Switch

Maxxim Medical

Maytag

McDATA Corporation

McKinsey & Company

MeadWestvaco

Mediacopy

Medtronic

Mellon Bank

Mentor Graphics Corp.

Meridian Automotive Systems

Merit Abrasive Products

Merrill Corporation

Merrill Lynch

MetLife

Micro Motion, Inc.

Microsoft

Midcom Inc.

Midwest Electric Products

Milacron

Modern Plastics Technics

Modine Manufacturing

Moen

Money's Foods Us Inc.

Monona Wire Corp.

Monsanto

Morgan Stanley

Motion Control Industries

Motor Coach Industries International

Motorola

Mrs. Allison's Cookie Co.

MTD Southwest

Mulox

Munro & Company

Nabco

Nabisco

NACCO Industries

National City Corporation

National Electric Carbon Products

National Life

National Semiconductor

NCR Corporation

neoIT

NETGEAR

Network Associates

Newell Rubbermaid

Newell Window Furnishings

New World Pasta

New York Life Insurance Co.

Nice Ball Bearings

Nike

Nordstrom

Northrop Grumman

Northwest Airlines

Nu Gro Technologies

Nu-kote International

NutraMax Products

Nypro Alabama

O'Bryan Brothers Inc.

Ocwen Financial

Office Depot

Ogden Manufacturing

Oglevee, Ltd

Ohio Art

Ohmite Manufacturing Co.

Old Forge Lamp & Shade

Omniglow Corporation

ON Semiconductor

Oracle

Orbitz

OshKosh B'Gosh

Otis Elevator

Outsource Partners International

Owens-Brigam Medical Co.

Owens Corning

Owens-Illinois, Inc.

Oxford Automotive

Oxford Industries

Pacific Precision Metals

Pak-Mor Manufacturing

palmOne

Parallax Power Components

Paramount Apparel International

Parker Hannifin

Parsons E&C

Paxar Corporation

Pearson Digital Learning

Peavey Electronics Corporation

PeopleSoft

PepsiCo

Pericom Semiconductor

PerkinElmer

PerkinElmer Life Sciences, Inc.

Perot Systems

Pfaltzgraff

Pfizer

Phillips-Van Heusen

Photronics

Pinnacle Frames

Pinnacle West Capital Corporation

Pitney Bowes

Plaid Clothing Company

Planar Systems

Plexus

Pliant Corporation

PL Industries

Polaroid

Polymer Sealing Solutions

Portal Software

Portex, Inc.

Portola Packaging

Port Townsend Paper Corp.

Power-One Pratt & Whitney

priceline.com

Price

Pfister

Pridecraft Enterprises

Prime Tanning

Primus Telecom

Procter & Gamble

Progress Lighting

ProQuest

Providian Financial

Prudential Insurance

Quadion Corporation

Quaker Oats

Quantegy

Quark

Qwest Communications

Radio Flyer

Radio Shack

Rainbow Technologies

Rawlings Sporting Goods

Rayovac

Raytheon Aircraft

RBX Industries

RCG Information Technology

Red Kap

Regal-Beloit Corporation

Regal Rugs

Regence Group

Respiratory Support Products

R.G. Barry Corp.

Rich Products

River Holding Corp.

Robert Manufacturing Co.

Robert Mitchell Co., Inc.

Rockwell Automation

Rockwell Collins

Rogers

ROHM & HAAS

Ropak Northwest

RR Donnelley & Sons

Rugged Sportswear

Russell Corporation

S 1 Corporation

S&B Engineers and Constructors

Sabre

Safeway

SAIC

Sallie Mae

Samsonite

Samuel-Whittar, Inc.

Sanford

Sanmina-SCI

Sapient

Sara Lee

Saturn Electronics & Engineering

SBC Communications

Schumacher Electric

Scientific Atlanta

Seal Glove Manufacturing

Seco Manufacturing Co.

SEI Investments

Sequa Corporation

Seton Company

Sheldahl Inc.

Shipping Systems, Inc.

Shugart Corp.

Siebel Systems

Sierra Atlantic

Sights Denim Systems, Inc.

Signal Transformer

Signet Armorlite, Inc.

Sikorsky

Silicon Graphics

Simula Automotive Safety

SITEL

Skyworks Solutions

SMC Networks

SML Labels

SNC Manufacturing Company

SoftBrands

Sola Optical USA

Solectron

Sonoco Products Co.

Southwire Company

Sovereign Bancorp

Spectrum Control

Spicer Driveshaft Manufacturing

Spirit Silkscreens

Springs Industries

Springs Window Fashions

Sprint

Sprint PCS

SPX Corporation

Square D

Standard Textile Co.

Stanley Furniture

Stanley Works

Stant Manufacturing

Starkist Seafood

State Farm Insurance

State Street

Steelcase

StorageTek

Store Kraft Manufacturing

StrategicPoint Investment Advisors

Strattec Security Corp.

STS Apparel Corporation

Summitville Tiles

Sun Microsystems

Sunrise Medical

Suntron

SunTrust Banks

Superior Uniform Group

Supra Telecom

Sure Fit

SurePrep

The Sutherland Group

Sweetheart Cup Co.

Swift Denim

Sykes Enterprises

Symbol Technologies

Synopsys

Synygy

Takata Retraint Systems

Target

Teccor Electronics

Techalloy Company, Inc.

Technotrim

Tecumseh

Tee Jays Manufacturing

Telcordia

Telect

Teleflex

TeleTech

Telex Communications

Tellabs

Tenneco Automotive

Teradyne

Texaco Exploration and Production

Texas Instruments

Textron

Thermal Industries

Therm-O-Disc, Inc.

Thermo Electron

Thomas & Betts

Thomas Saginaw Ball Screw Co.

Thomasville Furniture

Three G'S Manufacturing Co.

Thrivent Financial for Lutherans

Tiffany Industries

Time Warner

The Timken Company

Tingley Rubber Corp.

Tomlinson Industries

The Toro Company

Torque-Traction Manufacturing Technology

Tower Automotive

Toys "R" Us

Trailmobile Trailer

Trans-Apparel Group

TransPro

Trans Union

Travelocity

Trek Bicycle Corporation

Trend Technologies

ThMas Corp.

Trinity Industries

Triquint Semiconductor

TriVision Partners

Tropical Sportswear

TRW Automotive

Tumbleweed Communications

Tupperware

Tyco Electronics

Tyco International

UCAR Carbon Company

Underwriters Laboratories

UniFirst Corporation

Union Pacific Railroad

Unison Industries

Unisys

United Airlines

UnitedHealth Group

United Online

United Plastics Group

United States Ceramic Tile

United Technologies

Universal Lighting Technologies

USAA

Valence Technology

Valeo Climate Control

VA Software

Velvac

Veritas

Verizon

Vertiflex Products

VF Corporation

Viasystems

Vishay Intertechnology

Visteon

VITAL Sourcing

Wabash Alloys, L.L.C.

Wabash Technologies

Wachovia Bank

Walgreens

Walls Industries

Warnaco

Washington Group International

Washington Mutual

Waterloo Industries

Weavexx

WebEx

Weiser Lock

WellChoice

Wellman Thermal Systems

Werner

West Corporation

West Point Stevens

Weyerhaeuser

Whirlpool

White Rodgers

Williamson-Dickie Manufacturing Company

Winpak Films

Wolverine World Wide

Woodstock Wire Works

Woodstuff Manufacturing

WorldCom.

World Kitchen

Wyeth

Wyman-Gordon Forgings

Xerox

Xpectra Incorporated

Xpitax

Yahoo!

Yarway Corporation

York International

Zenith

ZettaWorks

References

American Society for Quality Control. (1988) *AQC 42nd Annual Quality Congress Transactions.* Milwaukee, WI.

American Society for Quality Control. (1987) *Quality Systems—Model for Quality Assurance in Production and Installation.* Milwaukee, WI.

American Society for Quality Control. (1987). *Quality Management and Quality System Elements—Guidelines.* Milwaukee, WI.

Anonymous. Business: a bad business *The Economist* (1999, July 3). 352(8126) 53-54.

Amsden, Robert T., Howard E. Butler, and David M. Amsden. *SPC Simplified.* White Plains, NY: UNIPUB/Iraus International Publications,

Bailey, Holly. The Tech Effect: The Computer Industry's Increased Campaign *Cost Computer Industry* (1999, Nov. 8), 5 (33) 1-3. http://www:opensecrets. Org/alerts/v5/ alertv5.33asp

Barlas, Stephen. Manufacturing Quality. *Managing Automation.* (1996, March), <u>2</u>, 61-74.

Bedeian, Arthur G. (1989). *Management.* 2nd Edition. New York: The Dryden Press.

Briody, Dan and Terho Uimonen. PC manufacturers await quake impacts, *Infoworks.* Framingham: (1999, Sept. 22), <u>71</u> (30), 8.

Butler, Howard E. and Robert T. Amsden. (1983). *SPC Simplified for Services: Practical Tools for Continuous Quality Improvement.* White Plains, N.Y.: Quality Resources.

Burrows, Peter. The Big Squeeze in the PC Market. *Business Week.* (1999, September 20), Industrial/technology Edition, 40-41.

Campbell, Tricia. Compaq tries to reboot. *Sales and Marketing Management.* (1999, July) <u>151</u> (7) 20-21.

Carlton, Jim, Deborah Solomon, Pui-Wilng Tam, Khanh T. I. Tran and Julia Angwin. Digits. *Wall Street Journal.* Eastern Edition. B6-7.

Costano, Anthony, Quality. *Journal* (1989, April), <u>4</u>, 27-28.

Daft, Richard L. (1991). *Management.* 2nd Edition. New York: The Dryden Press.

Dvorak, John C. The Computer Industry Slowdown *Net News.* (2001, January 3). 1-4. Wysiwyg://31/http://www. Ordernet.com/slowdown.shtml

_____ Have You Got Gremlins? *Net News* (2001, March), 1-3.

Faletra, Roberta. Is there no one willing to shake it up in this industry any longer? *Crn.: The Newsweekly for Builders of Technology Solutions.* (2001, May 7), Issue 944, 140.

Forman, Preston. Thin-client enthusiast expands business with simple solutions *Computer Reseller News.* (1999, March), Issue 833: 39, 42.

Freed, Les. Personal Computers: History and Development. (1995) *The History of Computers.* New York: Ziff-Davis .

Gaither, Norman. (1990). *Production and Operations Management.* 4th Edition. New York: The Dryden Press.

Gardner, Charles H. *Roadblocks on the Information Highway.* http://super.nova.org/ *Stories/Roadblocks/S2.html*

Geisel, Larry E. Knowledge-Based CIM Support. *Journal of Manufacturing Systems,* (1995, Jan.) 62-4.

Gitlow, H. S. and S. J. Gitlow. (1987). *The Deming Guide to Quality and Competitive Position.* Englewood Cliffs: Prentice Hall, Inc.

Gold, Bela and Gene McCarroll. Towards the Increasing Integration of Management Functions: Needs and Illustrated Advances. *International Journal of Technology Management.* (1998), 10-20.

Guth, Robert A. and Evan Ramstad. How Sony Turned a Skinny Laptop Into an Unlikely PC Success. *Wall Street Journal.* (1999, Nov. 12). Eastern Edition. B, 1-2.

Hamilton, Anita. Tempting deal *Time.* (1999, Aug. 9),.154, (6), 75-76.

Hamilton, David P. and Dean Takahashi. PC Makers Worry About Memory Chip

Shortage.*Wall Street Journal.* (1999, Oct. 4). Eastern Edition. B11-12.

Harris, Elana. Keeping customers happy. *Sales and Marketing Management.* (2001, April), 153 (4), 69-70.

Harvey, John and Gerald L. Page. *Journal: Harvard Business Review (HBR),* (1995, Feb.), 64. 69-76.

Hawkins, Del I., Roger J. Best, and Kenneth A. Coney. (1994). *Consumer Behavior.* 5th Edition. New York: Richard D. Irvin, Inc.

Hutchens, Spencer. Editorial. *Compliance Engineering.* (1991, Fall), 19.

ISO International Standards for Quality Management. (1987) ISO. Geneva, Switzerland.

Koehler, William. Production and Inventory Management *Manufacturing Journal.* (1993, May), <u>48</u>, 44-49.

LaMorte, Christopher and John Lilly. *Computers: History and Development.* http://www.digitalcentury.com/encyclo/ update/comp.hd:html

Mack, Ann M. Engage links marketing deal with Compaq. *Brandweek.* (2000, Sep. 18), <u>41</u> (30), 40-41.

McMaster, Mark. Making changes easy for salespeople. *Sales and Marketing Management.* (2001, Jan.)<u>153</u> (1), 74-75.

McWilliams, Gary. Shortages of an Intel Microprocessor Create Backlogs, Headaches. *Wall Street Journal.* (2000, *Aug. 13), 8.*

Mossberg, Walter S. Be on Your Guard For These 10 Lies As You Shop for a PC. *Wall Street Journal.* (2001, January 18), Eastern Edition, B1-2.

Mossberg, Walter S. Compaq's New Series Has a Quaint Old Look and Slick New Features. *Wall Street Journal.* (2000, Jan. 6), Eastern Edition. B1-3.

Munger, Michael. On the Flip Side: The Computer Industry is So Predictable *The Mac Observer.* (2000, April 11), 1-5.

http://www:macobserver.com/columns/   Flipside/2000/
20000411.shtml

Nance, Barry. Testing, testing…1, 2, 3. *Network World.* (2001,
Feb.19), 18 (8), 50-51.

Phelps, Alan. Mainframe to Mainstream: Computers Make
Their Way into Daily Life. *Computing Dictionary.* Third
Edition. (1998, December) 2 (4), 1-11.

Polsson, Ken. *Chronology of Personal Computers.* 1995-2001.
URL http://www.island Net.com/-kpolsson/comphist.

Process Management Institute. (1987). *Fundamentals of Process
for Quality Assurance In Production and Installation.* Milwaukee, WI.

Process Management Institute. (1987). *Fundamentals of Process
Improvement.* Bloomington, MN.: Process Management
Institute.

Rise Of The 'Wintel Monopoly' The, Smart Computing Editorial., 1-11. http://www.smartcomputing.com/editorial.

Robbins, Stephen P. (1991). *Organizational Behavior.* 5th Edition. New York: Prentice-Hall, Inc.

Sager, Ira. Bringing Mainframe Might to PC Servers, *Business
Week.* (1999, July 5), Industrial/technology Edition. Issue
3636, 88.

Sandbert, Jared. Why Combo Gizmos Don't Cut It—TV-PCs, Web-Access Phones Show That Whole Can Be Less Than Sum of Its Parts. *Wall Street Journal.* (2001, April 25), Eastern Edition. B1-2.

Schonberger, Richard. (1991). *World Class Manufacturing Casebook: Implementing JIT and TQC.* 3rd Edition. New York: Free Press.

Surviving the Next Operating System: Dos RIP: 1981, 1990, 1993, 1995,....*PC Operating Systems.* (1996, March 25), http://www.yale.edu/pelt/OPSYS/ Default.litm.

Thomas, Jason. Reactions by the Computer Industry to the World Wide Web. *Ethics And Law on the Electronic Frontier.* Fall, 1994. Papers/Thomas-comp-industry. http://www.swiss at mit.edu/6805/student

Toupin, Laurie Ann. "Virtual Assembly Processes Come to the PC Screen." *Design News.* Apr. 18, 1999. Vol. 54, Issue 8, p. 18.

Tran, Khanh T. L. Microsoft, Nintendo Gear Up to Compete For Sales of Their Video-Game Consoles. *Wall Street Journal.* Eastern Edition. B8-9.

Wasserman, Todd. 'Customer view' defines Compaq's branding tack. *Brandweek.* (2000, October 9), 41 (39), 10-11.

_____. Textbook Notebook. *Brandweek.* (2001, Apr. 16), 42 (l6),. 28-20.

_____. PCs unplugged *Brandweek.* (2001, Jan. 1), 42 (1). 24-27.

_____. Softness Yields CE Focus for PC Bets, Microsoft Plans Two Lines Of Attack. *Brandweek.* (2001, Jan. 15), 42, (3), 14.

White, Stephen. *A Brief History of Computing.* 1996-2001. 1-3. http://www.ox compsoc.net/-swhite/history: html

Zarley, Craig and Joseph F. Kovar. IBM Reaches Out. *Cm. : The Newsweekly For Builders of Technology Solutions.* (2001, Feb. 26), Issue 934: 14-18.

Zikmund, William G. (1992). *Business Research Methods.* 3rd Edition. New York: The Dryden Press.

Anthony J. Dennis (2003). Osama Bin Laden: A Psychological and Political Portrait.

Morgan Norval (2004). Triumph of Disorder: Islamic fundamentalism, the new face of war.

Note: (2005). Yonah Alexander. The Propaganda matrix-Exposing the New World Order and Government. "...to shape a New world order based on trade and a globalized economy." • Taiwan denounces Chinese 'terrorism'•

Note: (2005). Yonah Alexander is an expert on terrorism, he is an Editor on many books relating to terrorism: Terrorism and Business; the impact of September 11, 2001. By Dean C. Alexander. June 2002, Palestinian Religions.

Yonah Alexander (2004). Terrorism; Hamas and Islamic Jihad.

Yonah Alexander and Michael S. Swetnam (2004). Cyber Terrorism and Information Warfare; Threats and responses.

978-0-595-35163-3
0-595-35163-8